THE BEST AT BE

By Rose Murray Ro

Contents

First published in 1991 by
Print Origination (NW) Limited
Stephenson Way
Formby, Liverpool L37 8EG

     ISBN 0 903348 28 4

Typeset in 11pt Garamond by
Print Origination (NW) Limited Formby, Liverpool L37 8EG
Printed and bound in Britain by Billings & Sons Limited Worcester

Chapter 1

The Auction

Thirteen year old Sarah made a pretty picture as she sat reading beneath the bay windows, pale sunlight caught the waist length chestnut ringlets as they cascaded on to her almost grown up velvet dress, an inch or so of white petticoat edging peeped above her very first pair of real silk stockings, the most modern of cuban heeled shoes almost touched the floor.

On hearing screams of laughter she hurriedly lay aside her book on french literature and joined her family in the rose garden.

Sam Swanson dropped on all fours and sent Sarah's younger brothers and sisters squealing with delighted terror when he imitated a lion's ferocious roar, his beautiful wife Edith smiled as she reproved him for over exciting the children.

As the big laughing man rose to his feet Sarah ran to him, he immediately burst into song and gathering her in his arms he danced her polka fashion across the wide lawn. Sarah looked up with adoration, she loved him so very much, he was always happy, exciting, especially this leave.

Master of his own ship, Sam had decided to sell the freighter and retire from seafaring, although his father and his father before him had spent a lifetime seafaring he was determined to end the heartache which seemed to increase with each parting, his adoring wife and children were overjoyed with this decision.

Sarah, the eldest of five children had hung on to her father's every word, his joy was infectious when he related how he had signed a contract to freight an exceptionally profitable cargo, the money from the sale of the ship with the proceeds of his final trip would leave the family financially independent.

Rushed arrangements caused great excitement, an auction was speedily arranged, all but the families immediate essentials went under the hammer; people travelled from surrounding villages to buy up the treasures Sam had collected from all over the world.

Edith was tearful until Sam's soothing voice reminded her of their wonderful future; he explained the cash from the sales was needed urgently for vital alterations to the ship if he was to eventually secure the asking price, a deal had already been struck with a large freighter company, the details would be finalised on his return.

Still Edith wandered about, all her most treasured possessions were being snapped up, each one held its own little story, she remembered every detail of where and when Sam had given them to her.

The sale of their cottage brought a few gasps from the crowd; the bidding turned to drama as a wealthy farmer bid against a church representative, to Sam's delight the determined bidding almost doubled his expectations, the church had long since been desperate in their need to find suitable accommodation to house a pastor and his family. Edith was pleased when the church finally proved successful.

The families departure resulted in a carnival atmosphere when all the villagers turned up to wave them goodbye, laughter was mixed with a few tears, all good wishes were sincere for the whole family were held in high esteem.

A long but enjoyable train journey brought the excited family to Liverpool. The children were delighted when their father hired a couple of horse drawn carriages; the short journey brought cries of dismay from the younger children but Sarah was held spellbound, the hotel was huge, the white stippled concrete unmarked, from where she sat a section of the interior's splendour could be seen, her father had booked a whole front first floor suite. Overcoming awe Sarah was delighted at the thought of living in this fairy tale palace for three whole months.

A porter sprang into action, he raced down the steps and almost bowed as he opened the carriage door, "Welcome to the Adelphi. Good afternoon Sir, Madam, my name is Jevons, head porter sir." He gushed over the children as he helped in their safe descent from the carriage, "No need to trouble yourself with the luggage sir, I will see to that, and if you care to go straight indoors sir I will also attend to the drivers."

Sarah wondered why the two coach drivers suddenly scowled at the nice Mr. Jevons, she wasn't to know the coachmen knew that their expected tip would not now be forthcoming or that the coach tariffs would show almost doubled on her father's hotel account. Jevons dropped his smile as he ordered a team of bell boys to deal with the luggage, then he hovered about the family until they reached their suite.

"Anything at all you require sir, I will deem it a pleasure to do your bidding."

Sarah watched as her father pressed a half sovereign into the man's eager hand, only then did he seem willing to leave the family alone to explore their surroundings.

It was absolute heaven, each member of the family had their own bedroom, there were two bathrooms and Edith was delighted to find the tastefully furnished lounge boasted a well tuned piano; she would continue with the children's lessons and follow her usual practice of playing love airs while thinking of her beloved voyaging husband. Use of the dining room was optional, food would be served in the privacy of their suite if so desired. The reserved staff unwound where the children were concerned, smiles became frequent when it was realised the expected spoilt rich unbearable little monsters proved themselves to be delightful, well mannered children.

Although well bred Sarah was unused to people jumping to her every whim, she felt quite grown up when waiters respectfully held out her chair. No-one seemed to mind when she explored the hotel on her first day there, she had crept fearfully down a rear deserted stairway, she peeped into the kitchen, an irate chef was charmed when Sarah apologised in fluent french, the delighted man's mother tongue. All chefs have their favourites and Sarah acquired this status immediately. Her happiness reached its peak when it was considered Sarah was old enough now to join the grown ups in the ballroom, she was ecstatic, the large crystal chandeliers which were mirrored throughout the spacious room held her entranced.

Wonderful days were spent sightseeing, a ferry boat ride enabled them a fuller view of the waterfront's excellent skyline, the steepled parish church of St. Nicholas was dwarfed by the magnificence of the Royal Liver Building, from the top of which wing spreading cormorants seemed ready for flight, perhaps to circle above the Cunard premises before going on to land on the domed perfection of the Mersey Docks and Harbour Board building. Sarah later raced her father up the great crinolene steps which skirted the impressive William Brown St. Library. Breathlessly her eager eyes scanned the view, immediately before the steps she had just completed were two beautiful couples cast in bronze, sitting back to back they formed a centre piece to the ornate steble fountain, eternal loveliness had been captured in the daring nakedness of breasts; the perfection of the ladies expertly coiled tresses promoted the thirteen year old to decide her own hair would be dressed in the same fashion when she was older. Across the road to the right stood the vast St. George's Hall, its artistic mosaic flooring proved a highlight to the tourists. The staunch pillars outside towered over a wide plateau which presented a fit setting for the architects magnificence, a busy road divided the hall from the breathtaking view of horse drawn carriages which glided by against a backdrop of the impressive station hotel building.

As Sam's arm encircled the youngster's shoulders she breathed out.

"Look father it's just like a pretty picture postcard," her large amber eyes looked up at him appealingly, "can we live here forever?"

Laughter greeted her request.

"Those pretty eyes have much more to see, three months my precious will see the start of wonders beyond your imagination."

A musical evening preceeded Sam's departure, he had
admitted the thoughts of such pastimes helped ward off home
sickness while he sailed the high seas. As Edith's tremulous
voice ended the sweet rendering of a romantic ballad he kissed
her tenderly, tender whisperings were exchanged as Sam pinned
a surprise present to the silken folds of her dress.

The ever curious Sarah later found the letters E and S had been
fashioned into gold entwined hearts, she went to bed that night
thinking life was so romantic for older people.

Sam's leaving was a happy event, even he was jubilant, all
knew the sooner he sailed the nearer his home-coming.

The helpful Jevons fervently pledged his services, management and staff joined Edith as the happy captain made his final
farewells. As the coach speeding him away disappeared from
sight he was still waving and happily blowing kisses to a row of
small faces which lined the first floor windows.

During the next few weeks Sarah spent many happy hours
horse trotting the esplanade which divided Princes Ave. from
Princes Rd., either side was banked by tall Victorian houses,
only the rich could afford to reside in this district. Sarah enjoyed
watching the starch aproned maids flirt with young constables
or the more handsome of tradesmen, she had once witnessed a
couple kissing before parting at the gate, she supposed they were
married.

The end of the walkway opened on to Princes Park; entering
the tall iron gates Sarah would gallop the sweeping expanse of
grassland to her hearts content. It was after spending one such
pleasant afternoon that Sarah returned to find the apartment
unnaturally quiet. On entering the lounge she found two solemn
looking visitors, her mother unusually pale did not offer her
usual smiling greeting, instead she sat rigid, eyes unseeing. One
of the two gentlemen approached Sarah, his whispered words
told her of her father's lack of response to repeated signals, last
contact was made three days before his scheduled port of call
and unloading of cargo.

The men's parting words brought little comfort to the mother
and daughter.

"This may prove a temporary set back, the new fangled signal equipment often causes unnecessary concern, God willing perhaps our next visit will bring you happier tidings."

After seeing the visitors out Sarah returned to find her mother in a trance-like state, whispered words of the youngster's belief her father would return safely went unheeded, the unblinking eyes just stared into space.

Sarah sought help from the hotel manager, who quickly assigned a maid to assist Sarah in caring for the children. Long carriage rides became an every day occurrence while their shocked mother sat in a darkened room awaiting news.

As the days laboured by an icyness of fear enveloped Sarah; the daily outings often included a ride on the overhead railway, the train would carry the children the full length of Liverpool's dockland, Sarah would gaze across the Mersey and out to the waters past the Bar, she would send up silent prayers beseeching God to return her father safely.

Ten days had gone by when the visitors returned, Sarah was heartbroken when she saw their expressions. Seeing them into the lounge she hovered about the partly opened door fearful the children may barge in, the men's solemn voices carried out to the hall.

"A thorough search of the ship's route has proved unsuccessful, we are very sorry to have to tell you the ship has been listed as lost with all hands."

Sarah knew she must resist the urge to scream and scream and scream, instead she sank to her knees and burying her face in the rich material of her skirt, she sobbed quietly "father, father, oh father."

The next few weeks brought a lot of comings and goings from the suite, Edith remained impassive throughout the visits, conversation did not penetrate her trance-like state. Sarah listened as it was explained to her mother that Captain Swanson, for some reason known only to himself, had omitted to increase the insurance to cover his last special consignment, the remaining insurance should be paid to the owners of the cargo to cover some of their loss. As documents were presented Edith signed them devoid of interest.

Gradually the visits ended, then a week later Edith was informed by a regretful management her stay at the hotel had only one week to run. Still dry-eyed Edith received the news without emotion, the seriousness of her position did not seem to penetrate, it was left to Sarah to race about frantically seeking a place to move into.

The hotel's kitchen was rife with the rumour the Captain had left his family penniless; the family's woe left Jevons unconcerned, he was notable in his absence now there was no sign of remuneration. The more feeling staff were in no position to offer help, only the chef gave Sarah a glimmer of hope, he escorted the young lady to a street only a few hundred yards from the Adelphi, there the landlord of a rooming house agreed to let two top floor rooms to the family. Sarah looked in distaste as the seedy landlord scratched his head, the glimpse of the interior of the house brought a feeling of horror, but Sarah had no choice.

The sad eyed chef apologised for not arranging more suitable accommodation, how could he explain comfort cost money and he had not wanted to embarrass the newly bereaved family by finding them a place they could not afford.

Departure saw a changed Edith, the ecstatically happy person had gone leaving a sad bowed figure aged beyond her years.

Chapter 2

The Attic

Sarah was afraid she would vomit, she preceded the children up to the top of the house, her mother followed listlessly. The smell of overcooked cabbage throughout the whole building was nauseating. Her first act in their new abode was to throw open the windows, smoke billowed into the room; Sarah gave an exasperated cry of despair, she peered over the window ledge, the buildings had been erected on a hill and the house across the street was one floor less, its smoking chimney was on a level with the open window, the wind carried the black belching fumes straight into the already grotty room. Quickly closing the windows she looked about her, badly stained wallpaper covered the walls, it had been partly stripped in one corner, the plaster beneath was brown with water stains, an old sofa with its stuffings bursting out was jammed against a wall, on closer inspection Sarah found it was hiding a huge hole in the plaster. A small table occupied the centre, its bare boards in need of a good scrubbing, there were two chairs, one was rickety and quite unsafe. She breathed a sigh of relief when she spied the oil heater, it was dented and old but at least it would heat the room; Sarah sent up a silent prayer that the heater would work once she found how to light it. The floor had no covering except for the dirt which looked as if it had been there undisturbed for years, droppings of candle wax seemed to be everywhere, the only form of lighting seemed to be expected to come from a lone broken gas mantle. As the children fearfully entered Sarah opened the door to the second room, inspection took no time at all, a large bed filled most of the space, the mattress was thin and not at all inviting, an old chest of drawers was the only other furniture, she gave a snort of temper on finding the drawers empty, no sign of bedding anywhere. They had needed a roof over their heads and that was all they did get, there were no cooking facilities, not even a fireplace. Sarah put on a brave face and went out to meet her mother.

Edith entered the room and sat down, she took no interest in her surroundings, breathless after climbing the stairs she gasped "Sarah, the luggage."

Sarah was pleased her mother had at last voiced some sort of concern, her mother had not shed a tear nor had she spoken much, she would give the briefest of answers or instructions but conversation seemed beyond her.

"Mother I will see to it, you rest awhile." Sarah sped back down the stairs to retrieve their trunks from the hallway, she was on her fourth and final trip when the front door opened.

"What have we here then?"

Sarah looked up to the most colourful person she had ever seen, the woman wore a bright red dress, her high heeled shoes were gold, blonde hair tumbled to her shoulders, two kiss curls were flattened down on brightly rouged cheeks, lipstick covered the laughing mouth and her eyebrows were plucked in two very fine arches above huge saucer blue eyes.

Sarah was speechless.

"Y' never going t'move in here are y' princess?"

The stunned youngster nodded.

"Oh my God, the old sod is going up in the world, he'll be wantin' more rent soon, oh my poor feet" the woman took off her shoes and leaned on the wall for support while she raised one foot and rubbed her aching toes.

"Come on princess, let's give y' a hand," she gripped one end of the trunk, "which floor y' on?"

Sarah found her voice, "the top floor."

"Same as me, is this all y' baggage?"

"No, but I have taken the rest up."

"And no help I suppose."

Terrifying Sarah the blonde hammered on a closed door, "Why didn't y' help the kid, y' miserable old get?" her voice shrieked out unafraid, "who needs y' anyway, come on princess me and you will manage, won't we?"

Sarah nodded, she suspected her new neighbour had been drinking alcohol, but nevertheless she liked her, her friendliness was a refreshing change from the morbid atmosphere that had clung about her in the past few weeks.

The puffing pair were met at the top by a tight-lipped Edith. The blonde ignored the stony reception and laughed.

"Oh hello darlin, I'm y' neighbour, d' y' need some help?" Before replying Edith bundled her daughter into the room. "No, I most certainly do not" the door was slammed firmly shut. Sarah protested, "Mother the lady meant no harm, she was trying to be helpful."

A reproving look told the girl further protests would prove useless, her mother had already assumed her silent state. Looking close to tears the four younger children sat quietly on the sofa, Edith had used her silk shawl to cover the seat beneath them, after a while she listlessly told Sarah the bag containing all the hair requisities was missing, somewhere along the way it had been waylaid. An exhausted Sarah retrieved the last trunk from the landing.

The next few days enlightened Sarah, armed with a scrubbing brush and plenty of disinfectant she found her quest for cleanliness was extremely tiring, water had to be carried from the yard. After summoning the seedy landlord for directions to safely set the paraffin heater in motion Sarah discovered the water could be heated by perching the bucket on top of it. While Sarah scrubbed Edith prepared the bread and butter cheese sandwiches Sarah had shopped for earlier.

On finishing her chores Sarah looked bleakly at yet another cold meal, she longed for the rich nourishing soup the hotel had served, summoning all her courage she quickly left the room and ran down the stairs, the landlord answered her urgent bangings on his door.

"Please, you must help," Sarah pleaded, "we have no cooking facilities, the children have not eaten a hot meal since we came here, we cannot exist on bread and butter alone." As she spoke the man wiped his nose on the sleeve of his filthy cardigan, this disgusting act left Sarah nauseated.

"Should be glad they've got butter," the man gave a rough unbelieving laugh, "only got butter have they? There's kids around here wouldn't know what butter was if y' gave it t' them."

"But they need a hot meal" Sarah ignored the taunts and persisted.

"Use the chippies then, or there's plenty of cook shops, my God, y' do some people a favour and they always expect more, use y' nut girl, buy the grub already cooked, less for y' to do," then he slammed his door.

Sarah went wearily back up the stairs, as she drew near the top the clatter of high heels came from below, she leaned eagerly over the bannister hoping to see the blonde neighbour, disappointed it was the woman from the floor below Sarah wondered why the blonde never appeared in daylight, when lying awake at night she could be heard giggling, and making a lot of noise attempting to be quiet on the stairs, there was a man with her each time she came in late, but all was silent by day.

Refusing the sandwiches Sarah wearily went into the bedroom and lay down, her mother's beautiful evening gowns were spread out in an effort to stop the children's bodies coming in contact with the soiled mattress, coats were worn for warmth by day and used as bed covers at night for the same reason.

The following day Sarah went in search of what the landlord had called a cook shop, her mother gave her a small amount of money each morning and accepted whatever food Sarah brought back. Sarah discovered a dish was required, so she sped off to buy a cheap soup bowl, on returning she found the remaining coppers were only just enough to have the dish filled with steaming hot boiled potatoes.

All sat about the table watching eagerly as their mother shared out the still steaming potatoes, Sarah closed her eyes, she had never realised how mouth-watering ordinary potatoes could be. The dish was treated with great care, each day now brought about a game of guessing what Sarah would bring back for dinner. Sarah became quite astute at shopping, she soon realised that the early customers had some of yesterday's unsold food put on their plates, so she would hover about outside peeping through the window until she saw a fresh batch being served.

The family carried on in this fashion and were growing used to the lack of luxury. Edith refused to venture outdoors, Sarah faced defeat and gave up coaxing her mother to take a stroll, it was left to Sarah to organize outings for the children. She became adept at dodging payments, she found it quite easy to board the ferry boat with one child after urging the others to mingle with the crowds boarding, once on they would keep on the move to avoid the ticket collector. Sometimes they would sit on the pavement alongside the tram terminus opposite Lime St. station watching the talented Mr. Codman's Punch and Judy puppet show, this usually ended in tears for they would have to leave a few minutes before the end when the collection box appeared.

Sarah enjoyed these outings but she looked forward to a couple of hours privacy each afternoon; sometimes she would walk the mile to Princes Park and daydream of her horse riding days, or she would stand on the corner opposite the Adelphi and relive precious happier times. It was on such an afternoon she felt particularly downhearted, it was her fourteenth birthday, her bewildered mother had forgotten, Sarah doubted the sorry figure even knew what month it was. Sarah tried to cheer herself up by remembering her last birthday, there had been much merry making, she had received numerous cards and presents, even her father who was on the other side of the world had left a present, it was a beautiful full skirted plum coloured coat with a shiny Paris label; it was the very coat she wore today, not as smart as it once had been but she had wanted to wear it today, it was her last present from her father.

"Hello Princess,"

Sarah whirled about pleased to hear the friendly voice, she smiled up at the painted face.

"How are y'doing okay?" the blonde neighbour was still colourful but this time she wore a pink dress covered by a well-worn short fox fur.

Smiling happily Sarah nodded, "I am fine thank you," she rushed on to hold the woman's attention, "I have looked for you every day, I wanted to apologise, my mother didn't understand, she hasn't been too well since father left."

"Run off with another woman has he? They are all the same princess, don't you ever trust anyone of them."

"Oh no," Sarah looked horrified, "he was lost at sea."

"Me and my big mouth, I'm sorry sweetheart, I didn't mean what I said."

"No, of course you didn't."

"Come on, I'll tell y'what, you and me will go for a nice cup of tea ay, how will that suit y'."

"Oh yes please," the thought of having tea outside that horrible house was sheer bliss, she fell in step as the woman made her way towards Lime St. station.

Sarah noticed that almost every man they passed smiled at her companion, she was pleased that out of all the people that wanted to be friends, the woman had chosen her.

The blonde kept silent as Sarah drank the tea greedily, she watched as the girl ate every crumb of two cakes, her voice grew more tender as she asked, "Things not going too well princess?"

Sarah tried to keep some pride.

"Oh fine, I am keeping very well thank you."

"No y' not, if you and me are going t' be secret friends, no telling y' ma now, well you've got t' stop telling me fibs."

The girl kept her eyes downcast.

"Cheer up, it's not the end of the world, now you come with me."

Sarah left her seat and rushed after her new friend, they walked through the station, past the ticket office until they came to the ladies waiting room, the blonde walked in calling "You there Nellie."

A voice replied "Half a mo I'll be with y' in a minute."

The attendant emerged from one of the lavatory cubicles.

"Hello Nel, I've brought me friend t' meet y', she lives in the same house I do, and like me she's got no bloody hot water, just take a look at her."

The blonde suddenly stroked Sarah's head,

"When I first met this kid the gleam from her hair nearly blinded me."

She lifted a few strands of Sarah's unkempt locks, and sighed "Look at it now, dull and stringy, will y' let her come in like I do and I'll see y' right."

The attendant looked Sarah up and down, a mouthful of uneven teeth were displayed when she suddenly smiled, "Yes OK, does she want t' start now."

Sarah wondered what they were planning.

The attendant disappeared behind a partition, Sarah heard water running, clouds of steam billowed through the doorway, the attendant reappeared.

"Go on, go in," the blonde pushed Sarah towards the door, "y' can have a good wash in there and make sure y' get plenty of soap on that hair."

Unknown to anyone Sarah's tears mixed with the running hot water, to feel clean again was the only but undeniably best birthday present.

Sarah's afternoon ended much better than it had started, most of her woe had been dispensed down the plughole, although she did not understand why, she joined in the two women's laughter when the blonde told her suddenly, "You call me Eve, it's not my real name but it's one I fancied."

"I know why as well" the lavatory attendant laughed.

"Go on then smart drawers, tell us why" the blonde queried.

"Y' called y'self Eve cause too many Adams were after y' apple."

The two women fell about laughing, and Sarah joined in for the sole reason of merriment, it was so long since she had felt so light hearted.

A weekly assignation was arranged. Sarah would look forward to the couple of hours spent in the company of the two rough but very friendly women.

Chapter 3

Goodnight Princess

Sarah raced up the stairs, they had been living in the house for six months now, she had learned to turn a blind eye to its depressing interior. Having just completed her once weekly all over wash, her appearance was reasonable, her hair had never regained its lustre but she never allowed this to worry her, she was just grateful the family seemed to be getting by. The few mouthfuls of hot food each day sufficed, their main beverage was cocoa, it was cheaper and took less preparation. Edith's main occupation was sewing, instead of the delicate embroidery she now used her skill in alterations; the children were growing, there were hems to let down, too short skirts and coats were converted to trousers, and every scrap of unused material was stitched together to make a mattress cover, panels of silk dresses hung from the string which replaced curtain rails. The main problem was Sarah, she was growing so fast her waist lines were creeping up to her armpits, to afford more arm movement she had snipped a few stitches beneath the arms of her precious plum coloured coat.

Entering the room her first task was to light the gas, late afternoons were growing in and the room was dark, her mother never seemed to mind the gloom, she was usually found just staring into space, the children playing on the floor. Sarah was careful to hold the match just below the mantel until the gas ignited, on a few occasions ignorance had caused the delicate covering to crumble immediately the matchstick came in contact. The table had been moved, it had been their practice to use the four trunks as seats for the children at meal times, it was obvious the sofa was now meant to seat the children from the table's new position. Sarah's quick eyes noted other changes, "Mother where are the other two trunks?"

Her mother did not answer.

"Mother please," the girl pleaded, "where are they, our possessions are diminishing, your evening bags have gone, also some of your jewellery, every week something disappears."

Edith's voice came quietly but firm,

"You are a good child Sarah but you must not question me in such a manner."

Sarah's voice filled with compassion, she bent down and kissed her mother's cheek, "Mother I am so sorry." Straightening up she changed her tone, "where is the dish," she looked at the children, eyes twinkling mischieviously, "who can guess what we shall be having for dinner?" Childish replies rang out, each voiced their particular favourite. Sarah left them happy in their guessing game, but as she sped off on her errand her brow furrowed with worry.

The following day brought a chance meeting with Eve, Sarah had just left the house intending to take a long walk when the friendly voice rang out, "Princess wait f' me."

Eve looked even more colourful, extra to her red dress she wore long rows of beads, they almost met her waistline.

Sarah greeted her friend with a beaming smile.

"Where y' going," Eve linked arms with Sarah.

For some reason the girl felt a comforting warmth from the simple friendly gesture.

"Nowhere in particular, I thought I might walk to the Pier Head."

"Princess y' going t' have t' drop that posh talk, y'll frighten people off from helping y', not that I think y' looking for charity mind, don't get me wrong, but it does seem fishy that someone who can talk like you do could be down on their luck."

Sarah smiled but took in every word.

"I'm going to a dance, there's a ship in, otherwise I wouldn't be showing me face in daylight, do y' want t' come."

She took the girl by surprise

"A dance, oh no, my clothes are not suitable,"

"Are y' joking, y' should see the cut of some of the girls, I wouldn't go t' bed in what some of them wear."

Filled with excitement Sarah allowed herself to be led to a tramcar, they rode for about a quarter of a mile and alighted outside a tall Victorian house. As the two friends walked up the path the strains of modern dance music filled the air, inside the lighting was dim but Sarah could see the room had been lengthened by the removal of a dividing wall. The small space for dancing was packed with swaying couples, tables were littered with bottles and glasses, a gramophone blared out near the dancers, the air was thick with cigarette smoke.

Eve noted Sarah's unease.

"Don't be scared kid, I won't let nothin' happen t' y'." Her eyes darted about the room, with a triumphant "come on" she guided the girl to an unoccupied table, almost before they were seated a foreigner approached Eve.

"God bless us, give us a chance t' breathe, can't y' see we're talkin? On y' way," Eve softened her harsh words with a wink "come back after." Then returning her attention to Sarah she said "Y' know princess your gonna have to do somethin' about that mar of yours."

Sarah was shocked "My mother, Eve what on earth do you mean?"

"She's giving her gear away, the other lodgers tell me the landlord's place is full of her stuff."

The foreign seaman was insistent, he returned to ogle Eve. "God you're bloody keen," she was laughing at him, then she said "Okay, come on," rising, she took the man's hand and made her way to the dance floor.

Sarah was stunned, why would her mother part with their possessions? She gave the matter a little thought then scolded herself, it stood to sense someone in the house was helping themselves, her mother never left their quarters, she hadn't any contact with anyone but the landlord. A shrill laugh brought her back to her surroundings, the drunken woman on the next table had risen to her feet and swayed to the music, Sarah looked about the room and felt sorry for her friend, she wished Eve could experience the splendour of a proper ballroom. Rising from her chair she attracted Eve's attention, making signs she was about to leave, she smiled as her friend affectionately blew her a kiss.

The walk back gave the girl time to think, by the time she reached the house she had made up her mind. On entering she made straight for the landlord's quarters, without ceremony she burst open the door and marched in, fury within her heightened when she saw one of her mother's beautiful silk shawls adorned his table. The man had been seated in a large comfortable armchair before a roaring coal fire, the bowl of water he was using to soak his feet spilled across the floor as he leapt up. "Y' cheeky young cow, don't y' know t' knock."

Undaunted Sarah spat out what she had come to say, "What are you doing with my mother's possessions, have you been thieving them?"

"Thievin' them, y' cheeky bitch, I'll give y' thievin' them," the man roared out the words, doors could be heard opening as lodgers strained to hear the raised voices.

"Don't you come in here accusing me of thievin', that stuff was given t' me in loo of rent. I've not had a penny piece from your mar for weeks, in fact I've parted with a few bob t' her t' make up the difference," his nostrils flared angrily. Sarah was astonished, her voice faltered "I am so sorry," she backed out of the room and fled upstairs.

The man's angry voice followed her as he stood in the hall, his wet feet marking the boards as he danced with rage "Y' know what t' do lady muck, if y' don't I'll tell y', out, that's what y' can do, get out, I don't have t' put up with cheek from alf faced kids, and another thing, I know y' all listenin', the gas will be turned off at the main from now on at prompt midnight."

Sarah fled into the room and banged the door shut to escape

the man's scathing response, she ran to the bed and flung herself down sobbing.

"Mother why didn't you tell me?"

The children were crying but Edith ignored them as she rose and went to her eldest child, her voice was calm and dignified as she stroked Sarah's head.

"We had to manage darling, parting with a few possessions is a small price to pay for survival," she sighed deeply "I have warded off telling you of our financial state as long as possible, you are too young to carry such a heavy burden," her voice wavered with emotion as she whispered "Sarah, we are penniless."

The following day found the figure of a young girl darting about seeking work. She marched into shops enquiring for errand work, she pleaded she would prove her worth at anything, she tried every stall in the market to no avail until footsore and weary she returned home. She tiptoed up the stairs afraid she would come face to face with the landlord, she was not popular with the other residents either since the man had suddenly raised all the rents.

Each day saw Sarah back job hunting, she remembered the market stall holders laughing at her request for work; one had actually told her she was so posh she could not know what work was, so remembering Eve's words she took her friends advice. and changed her approach. She entered a florist shop, the woman behind the counter gave a distainful sniff after looking the girl from head to toe, nevertheless she came forward smiling.

"May I help you miss" the voice was sugary sweet and the put on high-class tones made Sarah want to giggle, instead she asked "Would y' give me a job please missus,"

The smile left the woman's face immediately,

"No," the sweetness of voice had gone, "now get out of my shop before a customer sees you, you lower the tone of my establishment."

Sarah did not take rejection easily,

"I'll work 'ard missus, and I can print special cards f' y'."

The woman looked amazed

"Can you read and write," her tone was disbelieving,

"Yes missus, I'm a good writer, I can write in French as well." The shop owner backed away from the girl, not taking her eyes off Sarah for one second, she felt for paper and pencil on the counter and pushed them forward.

"Come here and write something,"

Sarah took the pencil and in her finest script writing she wrote:

Madame Reilly, Florist by appointment to H.R.H. the King.

The shop woman read with amazement, the change in her was unbelievable, an onlooker seeing the sudden haughtiness of posture would have taken the words meaning as truth.

The woman stood deep in thought for a while. Sarah kept silent, her heart was pumping wildly, she thought she might faint on hearing the florists next words,

"If I give you work you will have to learn to speak better,"

"I'll try and do me best missus,"

"And don't call me missus, my name is Mrs. Reilly, but in front of customers you will remember to call me Madam."

"Yes missus, I won't forget."

Sarah could barely contain her excitement.

"You will start on Monday, five o'clock prompt, I will not tolerate lateness, you will deliver orders, up to three miles you will go on foot, over that you will be allowed tram fare."

Sarah was in a daze as the voice continued on about a wage and stoppages for the slightest of damage, she made an effort to gather her wits, the voice droned on:

"I will have plain cards ready for Monday, any spare time you have will be spent printing them, now go away, and make sure you are tidy when you report for work,"

"Yes Madam, thank you, thank you," she had forgotten her accent, in desperation she disappeared through the door before the woman could question her lapse.

Sarah sped home to her mother, her wages would just cover the rent, they need never part with their few remaining possessions.

That night Sarah was too excited to sleep, she had work for six whole days every week, her young mind raced ahead, if she could find work for the seventh day they would have enough money for food. Her thoughts were interrupted by a noise on the stairs, someone was singing, the tell tale sound of high heels climbing the top flight brought a smile to the girl's face. Eve was alone and she was grumbling about the long climb up to the top floor, her speech was slurred, she dropped her keys, Sarah wanted to go to her friend but knew she dare not wake her mother and the children. Eve's voice suddenly rang out loudly, "Goodnight Princess, my lovely sweet innocent princess, good night, Eve loves you."

Sarah smiled into the darkness and thought I love you too, and what's more my dear friend when we meet at the Station tomorrow I shall tell you so.

The following morning Sarah started down the stairs with the children for their usual daily walk, she stooped to pick up a ladies handkerchief on the stairs, when she saw the smear of bright red lipstick she smiled, she knew who it belonged to and put it in her pocket, she would give it back to Eve when they met later that afternoon.

While the children played at the Pier Head Sarah gave a contented sigh, her success at finding work had snowballed to more good news; she had voiced her fears for the children's recreation, she would not be able to continue the routine of the last two years, her mother had put her mind at ease by announcing her intention of venturing outdoors. Edith had at last smiled when she chided her daughter for wanting to do what was humanly impossible, they had laughed when she pointed out no-one could be in two places at one time. Sarah reflected and decided this was the most contented she had felt since the loss of her father. She gathered her brothers and sisters and walked them slowly home, her happiness was infectious for the children laughed and giggled on their way upstairs.

On reaching the top floor Sarah grew alarmed, she sniffed the air, bursting into the room she startled her mother when she raced to check the gas, she dashed back out on to the landing sniffing as she went, her sense of smell took her to Eve's door; she tried the knob, it did not turn, panic stricken she banged with both fists on the door "Eve! Eve! oh please Eve wake up, there's gas escaping, Eve! Eve!" Her hysterical cries alerted the household. The landlord appeared with a key, he opened the door and disappeared into Eve's room, he turned back and attempted to stop Sarah from entering, but she pushed by him, she was filled with horror at the sight of her treasured friend. Still fully dressed and wearing the gold shoes Eve lay on the bed, she looked like a broken butterfly, merciful blackness wiped out the pitiful scene as Sarah fainted to the floor.

Lying on the landing floor she came too amid her mother's distress and the angry opinions of other lodgers. Struggling to her feet she ignored her mother's pleas and whirled towards the landlord.

"You killed her" she stormed, she beat the man's chest with clenched fists, "you killed her, you turned off the gas while Eve's was still lit, when you turned it back on this morning you killed her," still screaming Sarah was dragged away leaving the white faced landlord visibly shaken.

Although Edith kept the door closed she could not shut out the noise of activity from across the hall. The sounds drifted through to the fitful Sarah, her young mind ran riot, she blamed herself, it was all her fault, had she not angered the landlord by accusing him of theft Eve would still be alive, if she had not burst in on him he would not have sought vengeance by turning off the gas.

'Goodnight princess, my sweet innocent princess, Eve loves you,' the words haunted Sarah, each time her tired body drifted towards sleep the endearments would ring out, Sarah's heart was broken, sobbing could be heard throughout the night.

The following day was Sunday, Sarah did not resist when

urged to stay in bed, she thought her broken heart would never mend, she heard the voice of authority question her mother in the next room, then after the sounds of heavy boots descending the stairs her mother's apologetic tones,

"So sorry for her outburst, she was in shock, she is so young." The landlords gruff tones replied:

"Okay then missus, but you watch that cheeky little cow, she'll get y' hung."

The door closed and Sarah drifted into merciful sleep.

Chapter 4

Thank you kindly sir

Dressed in a warm coat, a thick woollen shawl about her shoulders, a cloche covering most of her hair and her feet encased in warm boots Mrs. Reilly gave the girl a begrudging look, there was no sign of approval at the girl's early arrival. She ignored the youngster's shiverings, the tear scalded thickness of the child's eyelids was noticed but not commented upon, the florist had no intention of listening to any tear jerking tales.

"Come on then, let's get started,"

Mrs. Reilly's voice was hard and unsympathetic, she pushed past Sarah and marched out of the shop. Feeling miserably cold the girl followed; she had risen quietly and without breaking her fast she had left her family undisturbed, she didn't know if her uncontrollable shaking was caused by cold or the apprehension of her first day at work. When her employer had secured the locking up of the premises she followed as the woman raced for an early morning tram. Mrs. Reilly occupied the side seat opposite Sarah, she scowled when the conductor handed her the two tickets, looking at Sarah she made her next statement sound like a favour.

"In future you can report for work by meeting me at the market, and don't be late, I've no intention of hangin' about waitin' for you."

Sarah's misery increased when she realised this arrangement meant she would have to trek three miles every morning instead of the few hundred yards to the shop, she resigned herself to an even earlier start to her day.

The hustle and bustle of the wholesale market entranced Sarah as she scurried after her fast walking employer, she'd no idea all this activity took place while the rest of the cities' inhabitants still slept, the visits to this hive of business were to become the highlight of her working day.

"Come on girl, we've got more to do than hang around here," Sarah was truly amazed at the different tones of Mrs. Reilly's vocabulary as the discontented voice grumbled its incessant harrassment. They left behind the fruit and vegetable section and entered the sweet smelling area of blooms.

Sarah stood by as a market trader became the butt of the florist's distrusting voice. The man served her patiently and showed concern when Sarah's thin arms were overloaded with the mornings order, he noted the girls trembling and the too small shoes which had the back uppers cut out to afford the blistered heels more ease, with his sympathy immediately aroused he was to become a memorable figure to a grateful Sarah.

As good as her word Edith had ventured outdoors and Sarah returned home ravenous to a hot meal, laying aside her own flaggings of confidence she made much of her mother's return to outdoor activities. Later Sarah enthralled her family with descriptions of her working day, she told them of the market and the beautiful flowers she delivered, she omitted the details of her disheartening day, like when her employer had informed her, all delivery of orders under three and a half miles would be made on foot or that two separate deliveries had meant a round trip of just over eleven miles without transport. She did not mention the laborious changing of water to all the containers or the freezing task of scrubbing the step and cleaning of the huge display window. Sarah was more than ready to lay her tired young body on the edge of the bed, sleep came speedier than ever before.

Having found a solution to their rent problem Sarah should have attained peace of mind, but unease still persisted. Having not yet met with success in her search for a second position, she wondered why it did not seem to matter, her mother miraculously still shared out their evening meal. Avoiding another rebuke Sarah kept her thoughts to herself. After much deliberation she breathed a sigh of relief (although it was tinged with guilt) on finding a quick search proved their remaining few possessions were intact, where the money for food came from was a mystery, the solving of which almost broke her heart a few days later.

Dropping the rough nasal accent little by little Sarah's voice was almost back to normal, she would conceal her smile when the strutting Mrs. Reilly claimed all credit for turning her employee from a street urchin into a reasonable speaking young woman.

"Not that you'll ever make a lady mind, so don't get ideas above your station. My father had class, he was a gentleman, he was a turf accountant, he saw the king once at the races, that's why he made sure I was brought up a lady, it doesn't come overnight, you have to be taught proper."

As a customer approached the shop door Mrs. Reilly abruptly ended the surprising revelations into her private life. Sarah was immediately banished to the room upstairs where she usually printed out the cards, the girl dithered and swung her arms about seeking warmth, she could understand the shop being kept cool for the preservation of the stock but this room above was unbearably cold. There was a heated room at the back of the shop but Sarah had been given strict instruction never to enter, the girl surmised the distrusting woman must keep her valuables in there. She did not allow her employer's domineering attitude to make her downhearted, for she knew the woman could never spoil the dearest of pastimes. Sarah had only to close her eyes and the flower's fragrance transported her back to the garden of their former home in the country, dozens of golden daffodils in the spring, and lattice work heavily laden with roses in the summer, snowdrops cheering up the winter were all hers never to be taken away, "Sarah! Sarah! get down here quick! that customer wants this bunch to be delivered to his home before he gets there, it must be a peace offering. Now he'll be there in about 20 minutes so hurry up now and get there before him, if we get this done for him he will come back again."

Bundled out of the shop Sarah sped off, out of breath she had arrived just before the man, having left the flowers in the arms of a delighted woman Sarah witnessed a loving greeting. As she retraced her steps she remembered her parents tender moments, whenever her mother's sweet voice rendered a sentimental ballad her parents would look into each others eyes until the words faded with a kiss, the tremulous tones were vivid in Sarah's memory.

The girl came to a sudden halt at the Adelphi hotel, she climbed onto a side wall and peeped through the window of the ballroom. As she watched the afternoon tea dancers whirl about she remembered her parents in all their finery, her mother's sweet voice kept returning as she watched. Suddenly she stiffened, bewildered she looked about, she was not remembering her mother's voice she was actually hearing it. A couple of steps brought the hotels entrance into view, the pathetic sight which met her tore painfully at her heart, through tear filled eyes she saw her mother, the four children sitting on the ground at her feet, she was holding her palm outstretched as she sang. An autombile had drawn to a stop at the kerb, a gentleman alighted, with a look of pity he approached the group and placed a coin on the singer's palm.

Tears rolled down the girl's face as she watched her mother call her thanks to the man as he entered the hotel, "Thank you kindly sir,"

Before the words ended an infuriated Jevons raced down the steps, his eyes bulged as he screamed at the sorry looking group, "Get away from here, I've warned you before you old witch," he pushed one of the children "go away and don't come back with your snivelling kids." As he returned to the hotel he shouted "Stealing the tips of a hard working man, that's your game you old cow."

The shock of the scene kept Sarah rooted to the spot, her mother had fled shepherding the frightened children away.

Now Sarah knew where the funds for food came from. She ran back to the shop determined to find some sort of an extra job, past efforts had not met with success but desperation drove her to vow she would save her mother from the humiliation of begging.

The next morning found Sarah waiting in the cold for her employer to arrive at the market. Knowing she had a while to their usual time of meeting the girl made her way between the stalls, entry had proved no problem as the gate man was well used to seeing Sarah every morning. She strolled the aisles aimlessly, the amount of vegetables lying on the ground had gone unnoticed by the youngster as she had been rushed by in the past. She picked up an apple and attempted to hand it to a stallholder, the man eyed her with surprise,

"No good t' me girl, that'll only be good for the bin now." Sarah looked shocked, "can I keep it please," it took all her courage to ask.

"Yes luv, any stuff out there on the ground is yours so when y' pass just help y'self, no need to keep asking, okay" he smiled as the grateful girl stammered her thanks.

When she went on her way the man looked after her young thin pathetic figure, "poor kid" he muttered.

Sarah secreted the apple in her pocket, she could hardly conceal her joy at the little luxury she could present to the children that evening.

A very irate Mrs. Reilly met her at the gate, "Where have you been? Think I've got time to waste standing out here? In future you can pick the order up on your own, I'll leave tomorrow's order this morning," she stormed off determined this would be her last trip to pick up the flowers. The long suffering market trader was delighted when told of the woman's intention, the thoughts of escaping her quarrelsome voice every morning brought a truthful promise from the man to send her nothing but the best of his stock, behind her back he gave Sarah a friendly wink.

The day would not pass by quick enough for Sarah; as she worked away the hours her young mind raced, she would ask her mother to make a bag, they could use the linings from the coats that had been cut up to make a bed cover, she would get to the market early and scour the ground for unwanted goods. The bag would have to have some sort of handle so she could carry it on her arm, otherwise she would never manage to carry it once she picked up the flower order.

The following morning found Sarah entering the market armed with the bag her mother had fashioned, the rope that had been used to secure a trunk was drawn through the top of the bag to enable the girl freedom of movement to manage the true reason for her presence in the hive of activity. She walked fearfully up the same aisle where she had picked up the apple, there in the same place were two apples, three potatoes and two large carrots, her wide eyes sought out the stallholder, he pretended not to see her, but when she stood there hesitating he met her gaze and nodded. She swept up the discarded goods and smiled her thanks as she put them quickly into her bag, this time the trader smiled as she rushed out of sight. Sarah could not believe her luck could be surpassed until the flower trader met her with a large mug of sweetened tea, she was close to tears thanking her blessings as she sipped the warming liquid while the generous man happily assembled the order. If Mrs. Reilly had known how much pleasure was derived from her decision she would never have made it.

The mornings happenings became a regular habit, Sarah was hailed by trader's calling "Good morning Sarah" as she passed by; quite a few of them made sure she had something to pick up outside their stalls, her early morning mug of tea soon accompanied a delicious hot slice of toasted bread, the girl's smile was to be seen more often, especially when she passed by the house and handed her waiting mother the bag. She knew she had put an end to her dear mother having to beg, for all they ate was what she managed to bring from the market. Cooking the vegetables had been a problem, the fruit and carrots were eaten raw, the potatoes were given to the lodger on the next floor down in return for paraffin oil, then without realizing it Mrs. Reilly solved the problem.

Sarah had struggled into the shop with the order from the market, as usual the woman began moaning the moment the girl arrived.

"I don't know what's going on, when I was collecting the flowers myself it didn't take me this long to get back, either you're arriving there late or that fellow's taking advantage because I'm not there, I'll go up one day and find out which is true, you mark my words."

Terrified the woman would carry out her threat Sarah crossed her fingers and put the blame on the lateness of the tram. Mrs. Reilly had begrudgingly allowed a tram ride from the market, the last thing Sarah wanted was for the woman to start accompanying her again, that would put an end to the morning pleasures.

Separating the flowers Mrs. Reilly continued "I want the window sorting out this morning, get everything out and be careful, I don't want anything broken."

Sarah set too, the window was soon cleaned, beneath the display ledge was a dark doorless cupboard, the dust was so thick she knew the corner had not been cleaned for years, she unearthed a large metal badly dented container, placing it behind her she scoured the dirt away. She was watching a spider running about, (its home had probably been swept away), when Mrs. Reilly cried out, she had stumbled over the container, "get rid of that old thing, get it out from under my feet."

"Where shall I put it?"

"Out you stupid girl!! take it with you when you leave and get it out of my sight."

That evening the unusual bangings coming from Edith's rooms caused the woman below to complain loudly. After knocking on the ceiling with a broom handle she shouted "quiet, let's have a bit of peace f' God's sake."

Edith was nervous.

"Shush Sarah, please stop now, the landlord might complain." Sarah was triumphant, she held up the container minus most of the dents,

"I've done it, look mother if we give it a good cleaning we can keep it filled with water, it will be quite safe on top of the heater," she cried out gleefully. "We can put all the vegetables in the water and keep it boiling, mother the children can drink the soup whenever they feel like it, you to, you should be eating more, the vegetables will do for our evening meal."

"The paraffin dear, can we afford to keep the heater lit the whole day."

Sarah fell silent, fear clutched at her heart, her mother must not go begging again, she forced a smile,

"Oh don't worry, I have that all sorted out, we are going to manage mother don't worry."

Her mother kissed her cheek and held her daughter close, "you are a good girl Sarah," then more lighthearted she laughed "and so clever too, where your ideas come from is beyond me."

That night Sarah prayed silently for a solution to the paraffin problem.

Chapter 5

Joe, the Jewish saviour

"Can I borrow your youngster Mrs. Reilly?"

Joe Silver was a nice man, he was the Jewish baker from around the corner.

"Well I don't know, she has her work to do here," Mrs. Reilly sounded as if she was being put upon.

Joe laughed and held up his hands spreading his fingers, "ten minutes I promise, she will be away no longer than ten minutes."

"Oh alright then, no longer mind, we are busy you know. Go with Mr. Silver Sarah, and as soon as he has done with you get back here quickly."

Sarah did as she was told and followed the grateful Joe to his home above the bakery.

"All I want you for Sarah is to light the fire, I set it last night so all it needs is a light putting to it."

As Sarah struck a match and set fire to the paper below the chips of wood and coal Joe thanked her.

"I wouldn't trouble you but the lad who usually comes in has started a full time job and can't do it anymore."

Sarah thought it such a simple task she wondered why the man didn't do it himself, then Joe surprised her.

"There you are Sarah," he placed a silver three penny piece in her hand adding "that's for you."

Though the girl protested her finger's enclosed the coin.

"It took me no time Mr. Silver, it's so simple, why do you need someone to do it for you?"

She was surprised and enlightened on learning the Jewish faith did not sanction toil on the sabbath day, this was the sabbath and Joe being a religious man abided by his faith.

Sarah felt the comforting three pence and said boldly,

"Do you want me to call every sabbath Mr. Silver, I would have to come while out with an order, but it wouldn't be any trouble."

"Good girl," Joe was pleased, "anytime at all Sarah as long as you come before the evening sets in," then he sent the girl's hopes sky high.

"The Rabbi needs someone as well, the same boy saw to his fire, go and have a word, tell him I sent you."

She flew back to the shop on winged feet, her prayer had been answered, hardly able to contain her excitement she waited patiently to be sent out with an order, she suffered agonies lest the Rabbi had already found someone. It seemed to take an eternity before Mrs. Reilly called her, for once Sarah was glad to hear the bossy tones.

"Get this order done quickly, I need you back here for another one, I'll have it ready when you get back so hurry up now."

The Rabbi answered Sarah's eager knocking.

"Mr. Silver sent me sir, he said you needed someone to light your fire," she rushed her words breathlessly.

The man was pleased, he looked kindly and his voice was gentle,

"Come in and thank you."

Sarah was ushered in to the quietness of his front room, looking about Sarah decided she liked Jewish people. Their houses were very clean, their furnishings good and sensible, not gaudy or flashy, the man handed her the matches and Sarah carried out her task.

Before leaving she came to the same arrangements as she had with Mr. Silver. The Rabbi brought out a little purse, it had a shiny silver clasp, Sarah's large eyes grew brighter when he gave her four pennies, her delirium of happiness sent her heart pounding as he said "Can you possibly go to Mr. Bloomberg, he is housebound, I know he would be grateful."

With Mr. Bloomberg's address tucked safely in her pocket the ecstatic girl sped off with Mrs. Reilly's order, she delivered it quickly then broke all speed records getting back to the shop. Mrs. Reilly gave a satisfied grunt when the girl arrived back gasping and panting for breath, she eagerly took the next order from the counter and sped off again, she went straight to Mr. Bloomberg's address.

He was an elderly man, a surprised Sarah found she could only just understand him when he spoke, the Rabbi and Mr. Silver spoke clearly but the old man spoke very broken English. After lighting his fire Sarah waited for her pay, the old man looked at her suspiciously, he spoke in a foreign language. Sarah shook her head and on sudden inspiration said "Parlez vous Francais," the man waved his hand in an ill tempered fashion, his quarrelsome voice said "Joe Silver," he then placed two pennies on the table, then he said "Rabbi" and placed two coins a distance away from the others.

Sarah shook her head and said "No Mr. Silver three pence," she held up three fingers, "Rabbi, four pence," she held up four finger's, she laughed aloud when the old man grunted and begrudgingly gave her three pence. Not having the time to explain and get the old fellow to understand the arrangements she sped off on her errand, she decided to ask the Rabbi to explain the agreement to Mr. Bloomberg.

Sarah spent the remainder of the day feeling very pleased with herself, she felt like a millionairess. On her way home from work she not only bought paraffin oil, she hired a can which she was allowed to keep providing she bought all her oil from the same shop.

It was fortunate for Sarah her predecessor had found full time work, for the Jewish people were kind to her. Joe Silver had observed the girl many times from his shop window, he had seen her daily with her brothers and sisters before she started working at the florists. He had first noticed the group because of their smart and quality cut clothing, it was unusual to see their class of person on foot, especially in the town area of Liverpool; at that time he was engaged to the lovely girl who had since become his wife. His mother and father had started him up in business, they had wanted him to follow them into the chip shop business but he preferred to earn his living kneading dough. When the shop next door to his parent's chip shop came up for sale they helped him to realize his ambition, he was happy, his wonderful grey haired parents were never very far away and the girl of his dreams had agreed to marry him, he was indeed fortunate. It was shortly after their marriage that he brought his wife's attention to the posh kids that passed his shop every day. Over a space of two years he had watched the little group deteriorate, the once smart children were becoming more and more like the dishevelled local kids, then he noted the eldest girl had started work for the florist, his admiration for the child was mixed with pity for he saw no matter what the weather her clothes or footwear never changed. He commented to his wife on the child's hard working long hours, he had known the three pence a week would be needed and appreciated. One Friday evening he was closing up when Sarah passed by, she waved happily to him, going outside he called her back:

"Sarah the shop is closed tomorrow and I don't expect any more custom tonight so perhaps you can find a home for these."

A huge lump filled the girl's throat when she peeped into the bag, it was full of cake, not the light teacakes she and Eve had enjoyed but heavy wholesome Jewish cake. Barely able to speak she managed just one whispered word "Thanks" before she fled off home. Pleased he had not offended her, Joe smiled as he looked after the fleeing figure, he decided he would make sure there would be a little of something left over every Friday from now on.

Monday morning found a chirpy Sarah, she walked proudly to the market, her thin legs and feet encased in large boots took on a confident march, she knew they looked too big and ugly but she did not care, the dryness and warmth brought a feeling of long lost comfort. Her eyes sparkled with happiness, at last all was well, her job secured the rent, the Jewish money bought the paraffin, they had a pot of vegetables simmering non-stop, the cake (sometimes) bread from Mr. Silver was a once a week luxury, and the tips from the deliveries bought a few extras. She had quickly accepted the offer of the boots from the Rabbi, they were not new but had plenty of wear left in them; she wondered where the bearded man had come by women's boots, she knew he lived alone, he had a portrait of his mother on the mantlepiece, perhaps they had belonged to her, she must have had big feet but the paper stuffing took care of that problem, she was happy, yes, she decided all was well.

Arrival at the market brought Sarah's cogitations to an abrupt end.

"Mornin' girl," the greeting came from the watchman, he laughed aloud on spying her footwear, "like the boots Sarah."

Unabashed Sarah did a comical little dance before calling "Good Morning Jack," with a wave she hurried off and busied herself with the search for discarded goods.

Taking the trader's whistles and joking compliments in good part she showed off her boots to make them laugh, but she did not dally for fear of angering Mrs. Reilly again. She completed the mornings business and rushed back to give her mother the food before facing her unsmiling employer.

"At last, you've decided to put in an appearance have you? I thought you'd got lost."

Ignoring the nagging voice Sarah set about her normal tasks, first she trimmed the stalks off Saturday's unsold flowers, Mrs. Reilly never wasted anything, one or two of the nearly dead blooms would be mixed in bunches of the fresh stock, they would be served to non-regular customers.

"This order is for a personal friend so be extra careful, don't let her find cause for complaint," Mrs. Reilly kept fussily rearranging the flowers as she spoke, then giving a satisfied grunt she stepped back and eyed her handywork, "there, that will do, now get off with it quickly and don't forget my business card," the woman gave a self satisfied sniff before adding,

"That'll make her sit up."

Sarah wondered what sort of person would befriend her employer, then after listening to the comments she decided the friend couldn't be much different to Mrs. Reilly if she was a fault finder.

The need for speed was necessary for the girl knew this was one order Mrs. Reilly could check up on. As she hurried off a carriage splashed her from head to foot with slushy snow, after frantically examining the order she glared after the now retreating horse and carriage. She wondered how she could ever have thought those filth spreading menaces were like pretty picture postcards, perhaps that's why her father had laughed.

With the business card secured firmly Sarah struggled on her way, it had become her practice to hand the card to the customer. After forgetting it on one occasion she had speedily returned and rectified her mistake, the act had been rewarded with a penny tip. After that occasion Sarah made a habit of forgetting the card, she would stand there smiling until a tip was placed in her hand, these pennies bought the luxury of soap for washing. On completing this mornings delivery Sarah returned speedily to the shop.

"There she is, the rotten little thief, I dragged her out of the gutter and taught her t' speak propley and this is how I'm repaid, the little bitch has robbed me, I want my money back."

Mrs. Reilly made to attack the bewildered youngster, but was halted by the shop's third occupant.

Jim O'Niel was a rookie constable, in fact it was his first day alone out on the beat, he took in the pathetic girls terror filled figure, he immediately transferred his commiserations, even he knew a thief would be better clad. As the florist made another vicious dive at the girl he roared

"Now just a minute Missus, hold your horses, let's hear what the girl's got to say."

"I helped her, took her out of the gutter and look how I get repaid, I'm ruined, you've ruined me you little cow!" she turned back to the policeman, "I want my money back, go on get it, search her!"

"Be quiet, roaring and shouting won't bring anything back,

now calm down and I'll start investigating." He opened the front door and with a jerk of his head he said "come on, you come with me."

Terrified, Sarah did as she was told and ran out glad to escape her employer's wrath.

Knowing it would be impossible to follow correct procedure in the florists presence Jim turned his steps towards the police station where a female colleague searched the girl. With a shake of her head she left the room, approaching the constable she sighed "If that is a thief it's the poorest one I've come across, look at her Jim, she's pathetic, there's not a farthing on her."

"Okay thanks," he entered the room and spoke to the shivering girl.

"What's your name love?"

"Sarah, Sarah Swanson," tears welled in her eyes as she rushed on "I haven't taken anything, Mrs. Reilly has never allowed me to handle the cash, if the money has gone missing from the drawer I didn't take it." As her words ended with uncontrollable sobbing the man's raised eyebrows showed his surprise. If the florist had taught the girl to speak she had done a good job, for the girl's speech was superior to the teachers.

"You're not a local, where do you come from?"

Bit by bit he heard the whole sorry tale.

"Will your mother be at home now?" His voice was kindly. When Sarah nodded her head he said "come on then, I'll walk you home and explain all this to her."

On the way he questioned Sarah about that morning's routine, the time she arrived at the shop, did she remember what time she left with the order.

When they arrived at the house Sarah rushed upstairs straight into her mothers arms. The policeman stayed for a while explaining, then he listened to Edith staunchly defending her daughter. By the time he left he silently agreed with her, but proving it was another matter. As he was leaving, the landlord who was loitering in the hallway looked at him nervously:

"Everything alright officer, no trouble I hope?"

Jim eyed the twitching figure and answered curtly "No trouble at all."

The following day Mrs. Reilly rushed forward to meet the policeman as he entered the shop.

"Did you get it, did you get my purse off that little thief?"

Tones of authority met the agitated woman.

"Madam, what time did your employee arrive yesterday?" He continued in the same manner, questioning her on their usual morning procedure,

"Now Madam, I've been led to believe Miss Swanson was never allowed into the room where you last saw your purse on a table."

"Never mind all that, have you got my money back."

"No Madam I have not, can you give me a good reason for the accusation you have made?"

"Good reason, good reason, that little guttersnipe pinched my purse, this is the thanks I get, I've looked after that girl, I gave her a job and taught her to speak propley."

"Did you teach the whole family?" His voice was cold, then losing patience he burst out, "I have walked from this shop to the address the girl delivered to, your friend corroborated the time, then I walked back. That girl must have run the whole way, the time she was away would not allow her to get rid of the purse if she had taken it. Remember I was here when she returned and you had already affirmed the time of her leaving, now you tell me, *did anyone else enter the shop at that time?*"

"No, no," the florist seemed to search her mind, "only the gentleman."

"What gentleman?" Jim let out a long suffering sigh.

"Oh a very nice gentleman, gentlemen often pop in for a buttonhole, he was very complimentary, said he had been on the look out for a good florist. I slipped upstairs to get him one of my business cards, I have quite a good clientele," she ended smugly "gentlemen always recognise quality."

The policeman gave a despairing groan.

"Did it never cross your mind that you left that man down

here alone, then after he left you found your purse was missing."

Mrs. Reilly bristled, "but he *was* a gentleman."

"No Madam, he was no gentleman, *he* was your thief."

"No! I'll never believe that, you tell that street urchin not to come back, she's not to set foot in here again."

The constable left the shop but did not return to the police station until he had visited Sarah's mother, convinced he had arrived at the correct solution he wished to end the families torment. His news was met relief, Edith thanked him graciously. Satisfied he had proved the girl innocent Jim left the house relieved but knowing the family would stay in his mind for a long time.

The front door had hardly closed on the policeman when the skulking landlord opened his door and raced up the stairs, he banged loudly on Edith's door.

"All right that's it, *out*! now get y' stuff together and get out," he sounded furious, "I've put up with a lot from that one," he pointed at a protesting Sarah, "but this is the last straw, I'm not havin' coppers roamin' about my house."

"Please, please listen."

He looked at the pleading Edith, "No missus, I won't listen, I mean what I say, get y' kids and go."

He raced back downstairs with no intention of relenting, he knew he would have no trouble finding a replacement lodger for the rooms were cleaner now than they had been for years.

Chapter 6

In the depths of despair

The afternoon found Sarah leaning against the smooth surround of the steble fountain; on leaving her mother with the children at the Punch and Judy show she had tried to assure her mother all would be well, she had promised to return when she had found a place for them to stay, she had no idea where to start looking, who would take them in while they were penniless? She looked up at the surrounding tall buildings, and thought of her father, without realizing it she spoke aloud, "please father, if it is within your power guide me, we are in the depths of despair."

"And who are you that questions God's power t' help you from the depths of despair."

Sarah swung around startled, she had not noticed the woman stop for a rest, heavy shopping bags lay at her feet. Sarah did not divulge it was to her deceased father and not God she had directed her plea.

Esther O'Halleron's ample figure almost covered the bench, she stretched out a pudgy hand and patted the small space beside her, "come and sit down girl, things won't seem so bad then."

"No I must go, but I will help you carry those bags."

"Now there's a good girl, but no thanks I'm only goin' round the corner," she gave the bags a scornful look, "only bones girl, but they carry heavy, y've got t' put up with that if y' want t' make a decent drop of soup."

The friendly tones prompted Sarah to seek the woman's advice.

"Can you tell me where I will find rooms to let please?"

"What's a thin little thing like you gonna do with more than one room?"

Sarah explained her dilemma, as she spoke she knew the woman was listening but her eyes were following the figure of a tall gaunt woman as she crossed St. Georges Plateau.

"I can't help y' girl but see that one passin' Georgies' All, well she might, hang on a minute."

The unsmiling figure approached, long legs beneath ankle length skirts took long strides, a thin scrawny hand carried a newspaper wrapped parcel, her red hair was drawn back severely from her face and formed a tight knot on the back of her head.

"Katie!" although her name was called loudly the woman kept walking looking neither left nor right. "Katie, Katie, Kate McKeva, will y' stop and listen!"

The figure stopped, she looked at the seated woman with annoyance, "What d' y' want?"

"Has Maggie Ellen got any empty rooms?"

"Who wants t' know?"

"This girl, she's got a mother and some kids waitin' at th' Punch and Judy."

"I don't know," the tall figure's answer was abrupt, but she added over her shoulder "I'll ask her," the long strides resumed their rapid pace.

"Go on child hurry up, go after her," the voice was eager, urging the girl to race after the retreating figure.

Esther looked anxiously after the fleeing thin figure, she silently wished her luck, the big honest eyes had won her heart; the woman had always longed for a daughter, she was blessed with three fine boys but a girl was never to be, she had liked the way the girl's voice grew tender whenever she spoke of her mother, she rose to her feet and lifted the bags then she struggled the same path as the excited girl.

A stones throw from the rear of the library Sarah found herself in a very different world to what her father had described as an architects inspired genius. She followed Kate McKeva towards a maze of streets, the second of which was Gerard St., having strode down halfway the woman disappeared up steps and into a house. Sarah kept close behind and stood hovering in the hallway outside an open parlour door.

Kate was standing before the imposing Maggie Ellen, the discarded newspaper covering lay on a chenile covered table. "This all they had?" The unappreciative words ended with a sniff, she held up a fine plump haddock by its tail.

"No Mag," Kate's voice was fearless, "but that's nice, y' know very well they won't send y' nothin but the best."

Sarah looked at the fish, her stomach rumbled, it was over two years since she had tasted fish or meat.

"What d'you want?"

Sarah almost jumped out of her skin as the woman addressed her. Without waiting for a reply Maggie Ellen turned to Kate "Who is she? What's she here for?"

"Essie O'Halleron was lookin f' a room f' her, y've got that one empty on Clare St."

Maggie looked the girl over.

"Bit young t' live on her own, isn't she?"

"Her mam's waitin' with more kids in town."

"I'm not a child, I'm fifteen and a half," Sarah objected to being spoken of as a child.

"How many kids?" Maggie ignored the girls outburst.

Sarah's voice sank to a whisper "Four."

"Oh no, no, no, no," Maggie Ellen was angry. "Kate where do y' get off landin' me with this? Now get her out of here," she turned her back on Sarah.

"Please, oh please we have nowhere to go."

"No, I said no, the rent is the last thing t' be paid when there's so many mouths t' feed."

Sarah was shaking.

Maggie eyed her, "Go t' Essie O'Halleron, she should mind her own business, let her give y' a room, she's got a house."

In desperation Sarah fumbled in her pocket, as she drew out a card a lipstick stained handkerchief fell unnoticed to the floor.

"Look, please look," the agitated girl ventured nearer and forced the card into Maggie Ellen's hand.

"That is proof of rent payments, we were at our last lodgings for two whole years and didn't miss the rent once."

The woman examined the list of figures, "Who did this writin'?"

Sarah looked surprised, "I did."

"Can y'do readin' as well?"

"Yes, oh yes, I am very good at both."

Sarah failed to understand why but Maggie Ellen suddenly changed, even Kate showed surprise when the woman said "Okay, y'can have the room on Clare Street, I don't suppose we could see little kids without a roof over their heads, now get out, I can't stand here talkin' all day, Kate'l show y' where it is."

Sarah breathed a sigh of relief, "Thank you, oh thank you."

Kate took the girls arm and dragged her from the room. Without a word she strode off up Gerard St., Sarah followed eagerly. Clare St. was but two minutes away, the room was cleaner than expected, a large double bed took up one half, while a table and three chairs were positioned by the window. It was the wide double hobbed fireplace that pleased Sarah most, she was quite joyful at the thought of living without the smell of paraffin oil, but she did wonder what the big hook was used for, it had been fashioned into the mantle piece and a connecting chain hung down before the empty fireplace.

With the key secure in her pocket a jubilant Sarah raced back along Lime St. Mr. Codman had long since ended his show and a worried Edith was relieved to see the return of her smiling daughter. Between dragging and pushing, the two trunks were taken as far as the corner of Clare St.

Esther O'Halleron sat on the steps, she gave a beaming smile on sighting Sarah.

"Had a feelin' you'd get it girl, hang on there a minute," she called out over her shoulder, "hey you lads get out here and give this poor woman a hand."

Three tall young men bounded down the steps and followed their mothers directions.

"They're in Maggie Ellen's place, opposite the washhouse door."

Sarah looked at the smiling helpers, they were all of smart appearance, none gave her a second look, but their willingness to help was heartening.

"Here let me take that."

Sarah looked surprised, the voice was devoid of the nasal Liverpool accent, his tone was that of an educated person.

"See y' later girl when y've got y'self settled."

Sarah smiled her thanks to the friendly Esther.

Later mother and daughter exchanged terrified looks when their deep discussion was interrupted by a tap on the door. The question of rent had not been mentioned, fearing a rent collector both were relieved to see a beaming Esther, she offered Edith a steaming tureen. Remembering her mother's reaction to Eve's offer of help Sarah sent up a silent prayer of thanks when the friendly gesture was graciously accepted. Without invitation Esther seated herself on the edge of the bed, she chattered happily while Edith settled the children with the hot nourishing soup.

"Y' look worried missus, what's up then,"

Edith took the woman into her confidence and told of their financial dilemma. With a wave of her hand Esther scorned aside their anxiety, "you worry too much, now tell me missus are y'desperate to keep them trunks."

"No," Edith was mystified, "why do you ask?"

"Cos them trunks is money, I'll show y'how in the mornin', y'll have more than enough f'rent."

Sarah and her mother exchanged joyful looks.

"Thank you, you are so kind."

"No, not really girl, the world id be a better place if we all helped one another more."

Esther changed the conversation. "Yiz all talk proper, that's nice tharris, my lads talk like that, I never got t'school meself but I made sure my lads did, they talk real posh like youse do. Our Tom, that's me eldest, was clever and won a scholarship, he went t' collidge and works for the council now, our Mathew and Mark are still studyin', but they're just as clever."

Edith smiled, she admired the woman's obvious pride in her sons. Long before parting she decided she liked Esther and hoped the feeling was mutual, the two women from very different backgrounds were to become firm friends.

Sleep came surprisingly easy to Edith as she lay alongside her younger children, but Sarah was unsettled. She was feeling the effects of the distressing recent events, though innocent she had lost her job, she grieved at the thought of never again sharing the market traders cameraderie and the stigma of being branded a thief kept her from facing the kind Jewish people. Even though she had been lucky enough to find new lodging she felt desperately unhappy, to relieve her torment Sarah crept out of the house and walked alone in the evening air.

Strains of jubilation caused the girl to seek out the source; she found Gerard Street a hive of activity, people were dancing and singing in the street, plates of sandwiches were being passed around, little faces peeped from the windows, she walked among the revellers unnoticed until nearing her landlady's house.

Maggie Ellen sat majestically in a high armchair in the entrance to the hallway, Kate McKeva was busy behind a beer laden trestle table at the foot of the steps.

"Here Kate, get that girl t' give y' a hand."

Sarah was horrified to find the flash of diamonds indicated

her, she found herself obeying Kate's demand to "Get over here." Pushing past the laughing crowd she was soon busy pouring beer from huge quart bottles. An arm encircled her waist, she looked up into the smiling handsomest of faces, laughing blue eyes met hers as he relieved her of a foaming glass of beer. He held her tightly and whirled her about, then his lips swooped down to brush her cheek, the quickly emptied glass was held up in a saluted thanks and he was gone, the dark curly haired figure was swallowed up by a following hoard of amorous females.

A weak-kneed Sarah tried to resume her task, she willingly stayed late making herself useful but she did not catch sight of him again. When Kate insisted the girl must go home Sarah shyly asked who he was. Kate threw back her head and laughed "Stole another heart 'as he? He's Edward, Maggie Ellen's son, this do is his send off," the big woman's face saddened, "his regiment is off t' Egypt in th' mornin'."

Sarah looked down at her big boots, and all the way home she wished she was as beautiful as the fountain ladies. She drifted off to sleep that night touching the part of her cheek his lips had kissed.

Esther O'Halleron was early the next morning, after cooking a big breakfast she waved her sons off and donned her shawl, then dashed off to fulfil her promise.

The journey she and Edith made was full of gaiety, the two puffing women laughed as they took frequent rests by sitting on the trunk they had struggled with. A boy with a hand cart was stopped to help and eventually they arrived at a pawnbrokers, while Edith looked at all the treasures that people had been too poor to redeem Esther haggled with the pawnbroker. She pleaded as if her very life was in the man's hands, finally she whetted his greed by mentioning the trunk had a twin and if she received a good price for this one she would most certainly see he got the other. A delighted Edith left with enough money to keep her family for at least six weeks, (she was to tell Sarah later, though Esther claimed she was uneducated she was a very clever person). Before leaving Edith purchased an unredeemed bedding bale, then tripped home happily exchanging light hearted banter with her new friend.

Having real sheets and blankets made the bed making exciting, a knock at the door interrupted the task. Sarah faced Kate confidently, the words Kate spoke were very different from what the girl expected.

"Maggie Ellen wants t' see y'," the woman turned on her heel and marched away, when she reached the front door she called over her shoulder "Now."

Mother and daughter exchanged a terrified look, both minds thought alike, had Maggie Ellen changed her mind, were they about to be evicted again? Sarah gave a little whimper and raced after Kate. As they turned into Gerard St. Sarah stood timidly in a doorway as Kate approached two fighting men, amid women's screams and crying children Kate dragged the abuse hurling men apart. They halted the obscenities when Kate roared at one of them, indicating the other who was covered in coal dust she shouted,

"What the hell's goin' on, he wouldn't hurt a fly, what's up w' y'?"

"What's up wi' me? I'll tell y' what's up wi' me, that bloody get asked my missus t' lift her clothes up."

Kate turned on the other, she was seething mad,

"Y' dirty little sod I'll kill y' meself."

The terrified man looked at the clenched fist that was levelled at his head.

"No Kate, no, listen t' me please, please Kate listen."

Kate halted the blow, the man's voice shook with emotion.

"I had a hundred weight of coal on me shoulders, I did ask the woman to lift her clothes when that bloody lunatic comes rushin' out t' batter me, Kate the woman was peggin' wet clothes on the backyard line, I didn't wanna dirty them."

The street audience screamed with laughter, Kate released the man and shouted "You's two wanna grow up." She gave a disgusted sniff and turned away, she looked at Sarah and said, "you, come on."

Sarah felt suddenly safer in Kate's company, as she passed the men she gave a smaller sniff of disgust then she sped up the steps after Kate and was left to wait in the parlour. She looked about the room as the door closed, it was vulgar with the crammings of prosperous adornments, an oval shaped picture stood out among numerous likenesses of the holy family. On close inspection Sarah could see the artist had expertly stroked the paint directly on to the bevelled glass, he had perfected a wonderful view of St. Peter's Cathedral. An ornate sideboard held a row of glittering crystal ornaments, all were under the cover of huge glass domes. Sarah looked tenderly at two crinolined ladies on the mantlepiece, she knew that the heads above the beautifully fashioned dresses would nod at the slightest touch, her father had delighted her mother with a similar set, a warming fire glowed in the highly polished grate. Maggie Ellen's entrance ended the girl's observations, the woman's face was sad, a none too happy Kate hovered behind her. Maggie's swelled eyelids were proof of excessive scalding tears, she sighed deeply as she seated herself at the table, parting with her son had proved heart breaking. It was only after drawing a deep breath she spoke,

"Now then girl, me and Kate here do a very good job of the rent collectin', we don't have the time t' write it all down so I've decided t' offer y' the job, I would want all y' writin' and sums done proply, no mistakes mind, d'y want it?".

Sarah was speechless, the woman's direct approach had given her no previous warning of the reason for her summons here.

"Well c'mon girl speak up, I said d' y' want it?"

"Yes, yes of course I do, thank you, thank you very much."

"Y'can start t'morrer morning."

Sarah remained where she was twisting her hands nervously, Maggie Ellen's last words were meant to end the meeting.

"Well what is it now? If y'want t'say somethin' get it done with."

"Will I receive a wage?" Sarah's voice was barely a whisper.

"We'll see, we'll see how y'get on first." As the woman spoke she eyed Sarah from head to toe, "have y'got any better clothes t'put on?"

Sarah shook her head.

"Kate, look at the state of her, I can't have her seen walkin' in an' out of my house lookin' like that, get her down t'Berry's pawn shop, anythink will be better than them rags she's gorron."

Kate pushed the tatty young figure out of the room, "C'mon girl, we might as well gerrit over with."

As they left the house a bleary eyed young man approached, his hair was dark, thick and curly. Sarah's heart skipped a beat, then she noticed the smile was crooked, his teeth uneven, the lines under his eyes were deep and sombre, and he had obviously been drinking.

"Ello Kate me luv, is Auntie Maggie in? I'm starvin' 'ungry."

"Y'wanna try gettin' in f'y'meals, she's inside."

Kate sniffed her disapproval, and walked off muttering "lazy dog shoulda gone away this mornin' instead of Edward."

Sarah gave a little sniff also, for she agreed with Kate entirely, from first glance she decided she did not like him either.

In Berry's the pair were ushered into the privacy of a back room. Not many people got passed the six foot high counter, but Kate was well known, she was always allowed in the back when buying up unredeemed jewellery for Maggie Ellen. On hearing the reason for her visit the pawnbroker soon had the dividing door unlocked. Sarah came out looking a different person, her happiness even made Kate smile,

"Let's have a look at y'in daylight."

Sarah whirled about smiling, for the first time in almost three years she had new underwear. The vest and knickers were thick and old fashioned but they felt comfortable, a long white petticoat gave a fullness to the skirt of an ankle length long sleeved serge dress, it was fastened by tiny buttons from neck to hemline, but Sarah's pride and joy were on her feet, second hand high legged leather boots showed off the true size of her dainty feet.

"There girl," Kate's voice was tender, "Maggie Ellen's done y' proud, you look after her an she'll look after you."

Sarah started work the next day, she found not only was she to keep up to date accounts in a big ledger, she was to accompany Kate on her rounds, she ran everywhere joyfully after Kate until the second week of calls. Kate hammered on a defaulter's door, a large chested woman swore she had paid.

"Y' shadder must have f'got t'write it down."

"Me what?" Kate's voice thundered.

"Y'shadder, she's always runnin' behind y'like a bleedin' shadder."

Kate grabbed the woman by the hair.

"Don't ever let me hear y'call her that again, and who d' y'think y'bleeding kiddin', that girl is too clever t'make mistakes so get the money outa y'pocket before I gives y'what for." .

"Awright, awright Kate, can't y'take a joke?"

The money was handed over, but Sarah was never to be seen running after Kate again. The big gaunt woman lessened her pace so Sarah could walk in comfort alongside her.

Maggie Ellen seemed to make herself scarce, for Sarah hardly ever set eyes on her. A message concerning wages had been relayed through Kate, the girl's family were to live rent free, the remainder of actual cash was to be held in payment for the new clothes. This arrangement seemed suitable all round except to Kate, (to Sarah's delight) she immediately returned to Berry's for a second change of clothes including a warm coat. She and the youngster had become more like friends and were often seen laughing together. Like the day Kate suddenly stopped walking and said "look at that," Sarah's eyes took in a picture of abject misery. A boy about three years old stood looking at them with big soulful eyes, his nose was running, his legs stretched wide apart with knees slightly bent, excrement poured from his trouser leg. A woman appeared at the door behind him, she smiled on recognizing Kate, "Hello Katie, how y'doin'," her eyes suddenly followed Kate's gaze and she immediately started screeching "Glor-i-er, Glor-i-er!!"

A girl up the street came running.

"Take Rudolph 'ome and tell y'mam he's kacked ees kex

again. Mind," she added in Kate's direction "she should be able t'smell 'im from where she is."

"That," Kate resumed her conversation with Sarah "is called after that actor feller, Rudolph Valentino, his sister was called after Gloria Swanson, their mam (soft cow) spent all her time carryin' in the movin' picture house."

They both walked away laughing but Sarah was suddenly thankful for her parents' foresight on choosing her Christian name.

Work was no trouble to Sarah, in fact she turned up most days earlier than expected. A smiling Kate met her one morning and placed a spotless piece of linen in her hand,

"Here, this is yours, it took me some time t'get that red rubbish off it but it's okay now, it's so pure y'would get into heaven with it."

Sarah looked down at Eve's handkerchief and felt silly for wondering if this was an omen, then she decided she didn't care if it was silly for she had a sudden feeling that her dear departed Eve was at last alright.

"Thank you Kate."

The older woman denoted a sob in the girl's voice, "y' a silly girl gettin' sentimental over a little thing like that, it's only a hanky I washed."

Sarah smiled, "Sorry Kate," she brightened her tone, "what are we doing today?"

"Well now, you and me will go and play havoc at the butchers an' then we'll call in at the market."

Sarah put her hands to her head.

"Someone should warn that poor man you're on your way."

"Oh it's all a game girl, we get things coppers cheaper."

They arrived at the butcher's window, and Kate indicated a large cushion of ham, "That's what I want."

They entered the shop and Sarah braced herself to watch the fiasco.

"Good mornin' ladies, saw y' looking at that nice piece of

ham, choice joint that, fit f' the king," the butcher beamed. His smile faded when Kate retorted "I was just sayin' t'her I wouldn't give it house room."

Then it started, the poor man weighed and priced every joint of meat in his window until at last Kate said with a wrinkled nose "How much did y'say that bit of ham was?"

The poor man gave a long drawn out sigh, "I didn't, but I'll certainly weigh it f' y'." When he told Kate the price she threw her hands up in horror,

"Oh my blessed lord no, thanks all the same lad but I'll go down th' road."

The butcher had no intention of losing a customer to a rival and immediately knocked three pence off the price.

Kate looked undecided then said suddenly, "Oh awright then I'll take it."

Sarah had to leave the shop before the transaction was completed, she was unsure whether to feel sorry for the butcher or admire Kate's wilyness.

They walked on to St. Martin's market in Scotland Road, they both enjoyed a big bowl of thick pea soup on every visit. Sarah felt Kate was trying to fatten her up, for the woman always brought out big chunks of fresh bread to be dipped in the steaming soup.

On their way back Kate knocked at a door in Lionel St., a young boy opened it, before anyone spoke a word he said "me mam said t'tell y'she's norrin."

Kate dumped her messages in Sarah's arms and pushed past the boy, bursting open a door and striding in she flung open a window to let fresh air into a foul smelling room, a table laden with empty beer bottles was sent flying, the whole street could hear a woman screaming.

"No Kate, please Kate don't hit me, I'll send the money up t'day."

Then Kate's voice roared,

"Y'stinkin' cow, y'd rather spend y'money on booze than on y'kids or keepin' a roof over their heads, now have that rent this afternoon or I'll be back again."

"Yes Kate, awright Kate I promise."

The two walked up the street with the woman's voice ringing in their ears.

Sure enough a rattle at the back door that same afternoon revealed the boy. Kate took the rent from him and told him to wait in the yard, when she reappeared she sent him off clutching a thick piece of bread thickened with layer's of dripping.

The next morning Sarah arrived to find Kate putting coal on the fire and Maggie Ellen studying the neat rent figures in the ledger.

An envelope lay open on the table, Kate spoke, "Is that letter from Edward Maggie?"

Maggie Ellen answered in a preoccupied voice, "Yes Kate, it came this mornin' early."

"What's he got t'say Mag, is the lad awright?"

"Oh Kate, don't bother me, can't y'see I'm busy, get the girl t' read it t'y'."

Sarah thought the two women must surely hear her heart thumping, she picked up the letter, she wanted to kiss the paper knowing his hands had touched it. She read the words in a dream world, he was well, it was very hot in Cairo, he missed all at home especially his mother, she would be pleased to know he was behaving even though all the girls out there were beautiful, he ended with a kiss for Kate.

"Can she read it again t'me Mag?"

"Awright, if she wants to."

If she wants to, Sarah repeated the words to herself, she felt the surgings of love beneath her breast, she would never take her eyes off the pages were she allowed to keep it. She willingly read the letter over again for Kate, when she had finished Maggie Ellen closed the ledger with a bang.

"That's very good work girl, keep it nice n' tidy," then she left the room, Kate quickly followed her.

Sarah pressed the letter to her heart and let out a big sigh, she was to find it difficult to concentrate on her work for the rest of the day.

Chapter 7

A little virgin

Edith knew her money would not last forever but she still had the other trunk to fall back on when she grew desperate. Essie proved a tower of strength, her advice was invaluable, she had told Edith to keep a kettle boiling on the hob whether it was needed or not, the steam was good for the kids breathing, and when buying a joint of meat never to choose a too lean piece. The meat was dangled on the chain before the fire, the melting fat could be caught in a dish and used to baste the cooking meat, and later the kids could eat it on bread. Edith was told of a Liverpool's test of a woman's love for her children, new blankets would immediately be cut down the centre, the two halves were then stitched together by hand, this practice brought the mother the comfort of knowing her children would always have a warm bed, for the pawnbroker would refuse to lend money on imperfect blankets.

Edith proved her love that same day.

Edith commented on people's cleanliness, although poor the men sported clean shirts, the women were never to be seen without a spotless pinny. Essie introduced her to the reason, they paid the wash house a visit.

After waiting in line for an empty stall both women were admitted, each stall had a deep wide tub where gallons of boiling water soaked out the dirt, a final scrub on a scrubbing board would bring the now clean clothes to rinsing stage. With some excitement Essie showed her friend a fairly new introduction, instead of using the laborious mangle, each woman tied her now rinsed clothes in a bundle and dropped them into the new machine, it spun them almost dry. Edith put her bundle on top of others and stood feeling sure she would pass out from the unaccustomed heat, Essie raced away to bring some cold drinking water. Suddenly a scream rendered the air,

"I'll kill her, the bloody cow I'll murder her."

Edith found herself being flung violently against the units, she was terror stricken. Essie returned in time to save her friend from serious damage.

"I'll kill her, the stupid cow's put coloureds in with the whites, me feller's shirts are ruined." the irate woman sent a couple of pink splotched shirts flying through the air towards the cowering Edith.

"So what," Essie shouted just as loud, "we all did it at first, it's her first time here an' I f'got t'tell her, be glad yiv got a feller t'wash f', the girl's a widder woman like me."

The terrified Edith made her escape and vowed never to return, but Essie convinced her all would be well and the next wash day Edith entered the washhouse nervously. While busying herself she felt sickened to see her assailant approaching, she looked about desperately for Essie, her heartbeat quickened in terror,

"Hello girl," Edith almost collapsed with relief, for the voice was friendly, "are y' alright, need any help."

Later Essie explained,

"They are like that around here, y'see girl, y' row was a sort of introduction, she feels she knows y'now, the barny is forgotten, you'll never have trouble from her again, in fact now she knows y' she'll stick up f'y' against anyone, whether y' like it or not, yiv got another friend." Almost in tears Edith wondered if she would ever understand the complex Liverpool customs.

Very different pastimes to those of her past life in the country, instead of flower arranging at the Womens' Institute and working delicate patterns of embroidery Edith spent most of her evening freeing the children's heads of nits, a fine steel comb had become an invaluable possession. Then once or twice a week she would accompany Essie to a game of housey housey, a man would sit on a box in the middle of Gerard St., shouting the numbers, the players would sit on the surrounding house steps eagerly marking their cards with an assortment of counters, bits of cardboard or even broken matchsticks sufficed. It was woe betide anyone who upset another's counters, very often the game would finish in violence when the caller would be accused of cheating. On one occasion Edith witnessed two men stripped to the waist shouting obscenities at each other, looking ready to rip each other apart they were hampered by screaming women holding them back. Essie had noticed her friend's concern and calmed her by saying "Take no notice, if them wimmen let go they'd both be scared stiff, they rely on their screeching wives t' hang on and save them gettin' a batterin', they'll be the best of mates t'morrer in the ale house." After that occasion Edith learnt to pass arguments without concern, she had more important issues to occupy her mind. Her main worry was the children's footwear, their original boots and shoes had long worn out, they were reduced to bare feet, but as most of the children in the neighbourhood ran about bare footed she had to come to terms with the situation. Edith grieved at the deterioration but was helpless to do little more than make sure they were fed. Every night she went down on her knees and beseeched God to return her Sam, her heart ached with longing.

Sarah walked down the street, she sported a new hairstyle, the day before a barber had arrived at the house to trim Maggie Ellen's curls. Kate had sat Sarah before him and ordered "Do 'er 'air." A delighted Sarah was given a fashionable bob, her brown hair had been brushed until it regained some of its natural lustre, the transformation was striking, all signs of childhood were gone, she was now a young woman. The large luminous amber eyes, her clear complexion and classic features turned more than a few heads, she blushed shyly when a young man whistled after her. The embarrassed Sarah was more than relieved to reach her place of work.

Kate was in the yard sorting chickens, she told a laughing

Sarah it was Maggie Ellen's way of seeing the kids in the neighbourhood got a decent meal at least once a year; any tenant who was up to date with their rent received a chicken, the size depended on the count of heads in the family. Kate passed one of the larger to Sarah.

"Here take that home t'y'mam later, leave it in the kitchen and I'll wrap it up f'y', now go through and make a list of who's t'have these flamin' chickens."

As she passed through the kitehen Sarah realised how clever Maggie Ellen was.

Every week one out of all the tenants received a threepenny discount for having the cleanest windows, this meant all her houses had sparkling window panes. The lodgers didn't realise that during the course of a year they had all had the honour to proudly parade the streets because they had been chosen. Now she was sure of all the rents being brought up to date, just by giving a chicken which had cost very little as she probably bought them cost price from a farmer.

When she reached the parlour Sarah was surprised to see Maggie Ellen with a heavily bandaged hand.

"Oh your poor hand, what has hapened?"

"Nothin' t' worry about girl, just a little accident, but it's stoppin' me writing t' Edward, will y' do it f' me?"

"Yes, yes of course I will."

So following instructions Sarah wrote exactly what Maggie Ellen dictated; she longed to add more, to pour out her heart onto the pages, but knew she dare not, she finished by addressing the envelope. Maggie Ellen examined the finished product, "very good girl, nice n' neat" then she left the room and Sarah heard her climb the stairs.

Busying herself with Kate's list Sarah ignored the opening of the door, a hand touched her hair, "Wha we gorrere then," the words brought the stinking odour of stale beer into the room. Rising to her feet Sarah quickly skirted the table, she stopped face to face with Carl, Maggie Ellen's nephew, he had moved just as quick and gripped her arms.

"Well now who'da thought y' was such a beauty."

Sarah felt panic rise.

"Y' gorra feller girl?"

A trembling Sarah shook her head.

"Y' ever had a feller girl?"

Sarah was speechless with fright, again she shook her head. "A little virgin," the drunken man giggled "I'v got meself a virgin," his hands came towards her breasts, she gave a whimper of terror and pushed them away.

"Give us a kiss then," her struggles brought anger, "y'do jobs f' everyone else, y'can do one f'me now."

He sent the girl crashing to the floor, she tried to scream but no sound came, he ripped up her skirts waist high, all her struggling could not prevent him from tearing down her thick bloomers. His drunken state and the girls unwillingness was making success difficult, he turned into a raving mad lunatic. Filled with abject terror Sarah raked his face with her nails, then suddenly the violent onslaught was ended,

"Get out of my house y'dirty little bitch." An angry Maggie Ellen stood in the open doorway. Sarah was still adjusting her clothing when she fled.

Evening came and the light was dimmed, Sarah lay in bed staring eyes unseeing. After screaming of her ordeal to her mother she had gone into shock. A worried Edith had hurriedly put the girl to bed and now sat whispering to Esther O'Halleron, she rose to answer a light tap at the door. Kate pushed passed the woman without ceremony, after placing a wrapped chicken on the table she turned towards Sarah, the girl sat up and held out her arms, "Kate, oh Kate" she sobbed. The big woman moved swiftly to the bed, Sarah flung her arms around Kate's neck and hung on tightly, the woman enfolded her in an embrace and rocked the girl to and fro,

"He was horrible Kate, he was horrible."

"Shh child, shh, I know, I know," Kate held the girl tightly and brought up a hand to stroke Sarah's hair.

Edith looked on in amazement, she knew Sarah enjoyed her

work, but she had no idea of the bond that had formed between the two, she looked helplessly at Essie while Kate whispered words of comfort to her daughter.

After a while Sarah calmed down, only intermittent sobs escaped her, Kate whispered "Now girl tell me, without gettin' y'self all upset, tell me, did he get y'."

Tears welled up in Sarah's eyes, she shook her head, "No," although whispered her answer was defiant, "no, he did not," the tears tumbled down her cheeks and she lay her head on Kate's chest. Kate breathed a sigh of relief and hugged Sarah close, "well that's somethin' t' be thankful f', I've already given the sod a hidin', but if y'd said yes I'd a broke his back."

She turned her attention to Edith while still soothing Sarah.

"You find a young man t'walk out wi this girl missus, it'll spread like wild fire she's a virgin, there's not many o' them around here, she'll be awright if they think she's got a feller." She returned her attention to Sarah, "I'll go now child, and I'll come an see y'tomorrow," she kissed the top of the girl's head and left quickly.

Edith was speechless, she looked from her daughter to Essie, then regaining her composure she said, "who is that woman?" She carried on impatiently "oh I know she works with Sarah for Maggie Ellen but, *who is she*?"

Essie sighed and patted a chair.

"Sit down Edith and I'll tell y'all I know."

The story that unfolded held Edith enthralled, her quick mind unravelling the complicated nasal accent.

It seemed that years ago there were two men, seafarers, they became such good friends that one brought his wife and only daughter Kate to live on Gerard St. Although a good husband and father his reason was entirely selfish, the two men so enjoyed their drinking sessions and schoolboy prankish humour they decided they should live nearer to each other so their practices could continue while on shore leave. Shaun Hayes (who was Maggie Ellen's father) decided because Shaun's wife owned all the houses in and around Gerard St. it would be more desirable if Paddy McKeva moved to Gerard St. Each time their ship docked Liverpool was their playground, both were good men at heart but both were mischievous; they played pranks no-one else would have dared, like the time they had a few drinks before paying their last respects to Shaun's departed uncle. It was the practice then (as it still is) to lay the departed out in the family's parlour, the draped coffin always kept open, a pleated sheet behind hid the fact that the covered window was kept open to prevent the room smelling of the dead. Mourners would sit in the room until closing of the coffin on the day of the burial, some were professionals and were to be found at every death bed. Shaun viewed the body, then, apparently too upset to stay, left quickly. Paddy made up for his friend's absence by bending over the coffin mumbling a prayer, the downcast heads of the mourners did not notice him slip a looped string around the wrist of the corpse, then slide the other end over the far side of the coffin, he then took his respectful leave. Outside Shaun had lifted the sheet and caught hold of the string, he made sure his friend was safely out of the house and standing alongside him before he slowly pulled the string. He jiggled it a couple of times before he heard the first scream from within, then all hell let loose, men and women came screeching from the house running blindly horror-stricken in all directions. The two then returned to the now deserted house and removed the tell-tale string. Essie laughed while telling this tale, she wiped her eyes before continuing. Paddy's wife was a beautiful woman, she put up with his childish behaviour and frequent absences because she loved him, she was heard to say he was her one and only love and would never want another. Their daughter Kate was a tall well built quiet girl, she was unfortunate in the fact she had not inherited her mother's beauty, instead she looked more like her red-headed father. She was a religious girl, so much so her father brought her a long heavy crucifix from abroad, she would be seen every evening with her prized possession entering church. Shaun's wife Elizabeth loved her husband deeply, but outward appearances showed indifference, his lack of business sense annoyed her, she would have rather had him stay at home to help her with the property instead of roaming the world. Their daughter Margaret Ellen was like her mother, quite pleasant looking in the face, but a little overweight and lacking her father's sense of humour. Like Paddy, Shaun tried to make up for his failings by showering his family with presents from abroad.

One night they almost frightened a man to death. One of their shipmates had spoken of a man named Joe who was pestering his wife during his absences, being small of stature he felt he had failed her for not tackling Joe who was a big bully of a man. The pair saw Joe one night, he was staggering home drunk, an hour later they crept into his house, both covered from head to foot in white sheets. Joe was asleep on the sofa, "Joe, Joe," the voice boomed eerily about the room. Joe stirred, and on seeing the two apparitions his mouth fell open. "You must pay for your sins Joe."

Joe became a shuddering mass of flesh.

"Me, oh Christ Almighty no."

"You have been found guilty of covetousness."

"What's that, warrave I done?"

"You have tried to take other men's wives, Joe."

"I won't do it anymore, oh God help me," Joe was drenched in sweat, "what cin I do t'make up."

"Go to church every day Joe and every time you go near a public house you must not go in, instead you must bless yourself three times."

"Yes, yes."

Joe by this time was a jibbering idiot.

"We shall return for you Joe if you ever forget, now close your eyes and say the rosary."

While Joe prayed they crept from the room. They had a whale of a time telling of their exploits, but Joe was never the same after. A mirthful Essie suddenly reflected sadness as she continued.

On one of their shore leaves Paddy's wife greeted him with the news, Kate had decided to become a nun. While the mother rejoiced the father was crestfallen, he wanted his girl to enjoy life not lock herself away, he became morose, no longer the carefree jester. On meeting Shaun that evening they both drank heavily, Shaun sympathised with his friend and both went staggering home.

About an hour later Kate roused her father with terrible news, Shaun's house was on fire. Paddy raced up the street to find a screaming crowd outside the burning building, the top half of the house was burning furiously. He raced through the front door and found Margaret Ellen unconscious on the stairs, having carried her outside he returned and rescued Elizabeth. With his shirt alight he raced in again as the fire wagon arrived.

After the flames were put out the firemen found Paddy with Shaun across his shoulders in the bedroom, both were dead. The whole neighbourhood mourned. Kate stayed with her mother, but the woman was never the same. The poor girl was worried sick, she was so quiet and helpless, she and her mother kept very much t'themselves, although bereaved herself Elizabeth tried t' make life easier for them. She was grateful for Paddy's heroism, and although she knew she could never repay the loss of a husband or father she made life as comfortable as possible for them. Then Paddy's wife died, (some say of a broken heart) and Kate was taken to live with Elizabeth.

Margaret Ellen and Kate were seen everywhere together, though Kate seemed to favour going to church rather than meeting young men.

When Margaret Ellen began courting Kate went alone to church. She arrived home from Benediction one evening to interrupt a robbery at Elizabeth's house, the brave woman was trying to fend off an attack when Kate arrived. The normally quiet girl raised her crucifix and knocked one of the men unconscious, then she suddenly went beserk and battered the other man so much it took three policemen to tear her away. After that she shed weight very fast and has stayed thin ever since, but that wasn't the only change, she became the fearless figure she is today.

Essie sighed, "that's why Maggie Ellen's house is crammed with ornaments, most of them are Kate's."

Sarah startled the two women by suddenly calling across the room, "What happened to Elizabeth?"

"I thought y'was asleep girl, Elizabeth? oh she lived for quite a few years after, then died of old age."

"Well why does Kate have to work for Maggie Ellen?"

Essie laughed, "Lord love y', Kate doesn't work f' Maggie Ellen, she does what she wants t' do, it suits her t' look after the stuff her mam an dad left, and at th' same time she sees t' Maggie Ellen. The money's provided by Maggie Ellen but Kate buys what she wants t' buy and it's never questioned."

"Well how can Maggie Ellen have a nephew if she was an only child?"

Essie noted the girl's sharpness, "Carl is not really a nephew, he's the son of Maggie Ellen's unwed cousin, he came t' live with Maggie Ellen when he was ten year old, he was a robbin' little sod, and still is f' tha' matter. Kate had insisted Edward went t' school from an early age," Essie laughed, "many's the time I saw her draggin' him there when he wanted t'go off somewhere with Carl. Kate hates Carl."

"And so do I" Sarah said quietly before closing her eyes in sleep.

The two women crept to the front door, Essie insisted the children should remain at her house for what was left of the night. She went home with a definite plan in mind, she would have to gather her sons for a deep discussion tomorrow.

Chapter 8

Blessed with friends

Tom, Mathew and Mark, listened intently to their mother's suggestion.

Sixteen year old Mark spoke first, "You are quite right Mother, the girl will have to find someone to protect her."

His two brothers looked blankly at each other.

"Are you really so thick," Mathew said scathingly.

"What have I done now" Mark protested.

"Mother is asking us to help."

"Oh," then added lamely, "I have my swotting."

"Does that mean you refuse," Tom spoke sharply.

"Well I would like to help, but my studies must come first."

"He's right," Mathew interrupted, "we have a week off, but it doesn't mean we can drop all our work. If I'm expected to get my certificate next term I shall have to cram all my spare time."

Essie looked crestfallen.

Tom sighed, "Alright, alright, I shall call for the girl this evening, we shall walk down Gerard St., and back again, that should do the trick."

66

"Oh thank y' Thomas." Essie was relieved, "I'll make y'a nice cup of tea b'fore y'go."

When she disappeared into the kitchen her two younger sons breathed a sigh of relief. "Phew, that was close, isn't Sarah the one with big boots."

Tom nodded, "yes, but she has had a rotten experience, I wouldn't like a sister of mine manhandled like that."

His brothers looked sheepish knowing he was right.

"Tell Mother I'll not bother with tea, I might as well get this over while it's still daylight."

He left the house and went straight to Edith's. When the woman answered the door she threw him a grateful glance. Tom smiled and entered, then almost immediately stood rooted to the spot. Sarah had slept better than expected, she was horrified when her mother told her of Essie's plan, with every intention of refusing the offer, she paid particular attention to her appearance, she did not wish any young man to think she was a waif in need of help.

"Good evening." her voice was firm, "I am sorry you have been troubled, no matter how well their intentions our mothers should not have encroached on your time, I am quite alright thank you."

Tom looked at the young woman who was very different to the figure of their first meeting, "Sarah, I am Tom," he stepped forward and held out his hand.

While she clasped his hand he smiled, "I respect your wishes Sarah, but I was planning on taking a stroll anyway, please, change your mind" he coaxed, "I promise just a short stroll."

Sarah accepted, she like the look of this nicely spoken young man, she felt at ease in his company, she donned her coat with a smile. Down the street Tom's brothers were peeping from the window, their mother wondered why they suddenly fell over each other to get to the front door.

"Tom, Tom, we'll come with you."

Tom drew Sarah's arm through his and called, "I thought you might."

When Tom linked arms Sarah did not mind, Esther's daily references to her sons made her feel they were already friends. She thought it nice of his brothers to lend their support so enthusiastically, but she knew there was little need of protection, she had grown up overnight, Sarah found she now possessed the confidence of an adult, she was astonished at the length of time she had remained naive.

The boys were wonderful, the many eyes which followed the group noted the attention showered on Sarah by all three O'Halleron brothers. The supposed short walk took three hours, the group were heard to laugh merrily all evening; Mark was the comedian, his antics kept the others amused, when he dropped to one knee and quoted part of Romeo and Juliet to Sarah his brothers threatened to pitch him over the edge of the Pier Head landing stage.

When they stood in the open air drinking tea Sarah remembered the times she had stood near this very place longing for a hot drink, suddenly she felt she had seen the last of those days. Reluctant steps returned to Clare Street, future outings planned by Esther's sons were always to include Sarah.

After promising to see them the following evening Sarah went indoors, she happily related the evening's happenings to her mother. Before drifting to sleep she thought of Kate.

The tall figure had arrived as promised that morning, remembering her greeting Sarah smiled.

"There now Sarah y' look better t'day."

"Kate," the voice was full of wonder, "that's the first time you have called me by my name."

"Is it?" Kate looked perplexed, then she shrugged, "well I can't keep callin' y' child n' girl now y' growd up."

"Yes Kate, I suppose I am."

The woman looked at her fondly, "Yes, y' now a lovely young woman, y' t' make sure y' gets y'self a decent feller, don't let me see y' out with no trash now."

"No Kate, I promise."

"Y' comin' back t' work Sarah?" Kate rushed on as she saw

Sarah start to shake her head, "no, I shouldn'ta asked y' yet, it's too soon, but I wants y' t' know he's gone, he won't be back no more. Maggie Ellen paid f' a train ticket so I put him on th' train meself, I know the rotten sod won't come back cos I gave him a good talkin' to. Mind, y' didn't do s'bad y'self, y' little tigress," Kate laughed gleefully, "y' ribboned the face off him," then she became serious, "y' t' take y' time, don't rush y'self, Maggie Ellen admits she made a mistake, don't hold it against her Sarah, she's not a bad-un y' know, an' old Kate'll miss y'."

"Kate, oh Kate I love you," Sarah hugged the woman fiercely to her.

"Go on wi y'," but Kate was not displeased, she continued quietly, "take y' time, don't let nothin' upset y', take y' time."

Sarah had nodded and Kate had gone off happy. Closing her eyes Sarah's last thoughts before peaceful slumber came was of her fortune, she was indeed blessed with friends.

The following week took Sarah like a whirlwind, the three brothers were seeing her separately in the evenings. Mark enjoyed the robust singings in the music hall, but Mathew took his pleasure from classical music, Tom was an outdoor man, he liked riding trains and sightseeing. Sarah enjoyed each outing enormously, not a lot of money was spent, for her companions were not men of means. Their mother was in the position to help out occasionally, her parents had had the foresight to buy their own house, (the very place the brothers now called home) and a few guineas had bought shares in a now thriving company. After the death of both parents Essie was sensible enough to leave the money where her father had put it, an annual share of interest made life more comfortable, her sons made contentment complete by taking a willing sensible attitude to education. She was fiercely proud her sons had not become yet more dejected figures hanging about street corners with no thought of employment.

Christmas was the reason for the O'Halleron brothers having a whole week off studies and work. Tom was employed in the legal department of the council, he invited Sarah to the annual party, she was delighted to accept. She looked a picture of happiness telling her mother until the visiting Esther mentioned the party was a swish affair. Edith noted her daughter's crestfallen look, and made up her mind to reward her Sarah for all the hard work that had meant the family's survival. She made a hurried visit to Berry's then rushed off to a shop in town.

Sarah stoked up the fire and sat poking it, her mother had been gone some time, she considered her situation and decided her recent whirl of selfishness must be eased down, she must make an effort to return to work. Kate had not visited again, she had been seen collecting rents, her eyes sweeping the streets but she had not approached Edith for rent. Sarah smiled on thinking of Essie's sons, they had brought her a great deal of happiness in their protecting roles, but she decided she must be sensible and avoid causing Tom embarrassment. Though she longed to attend the works function she would have to decline the invitation, her outfits were presentable, but they were unsuitable for such an occasion. Stifling her disappointment she greeted her mother's return with a smile.

A joyous Edith handed her daughter an expensively wrapped box, a perplexed Sarah carefully stripped the coverings, nervous fingers parted the inner tissue paper. "Mother," the one word was breathed in wonderment, then the boxes contents were scooped up quickly and held close to her chest, she closed her eyes and laughed, "Mother pinch me, am I dreaming." Edith hovered anxiously, "Try it on Sarah, let me see it on you." Later she wept when Sarah whirled about happily in the most up-to-date beaded dress, its shining splendour was out of place in the poor surroundings.

Suddenly, Sarah came to a standstill, one shaking finger caressed the radiant embellished beading, her voice was a broken whisper, "It's so beautiful, Oh Mother look, isn't it the most wonderful of dresses." Edith nodded, tear-filled eyes took in the beauty of her lovely daughter in her first adult taste of luxurious finery, and the dance slippers which matched perfectly.

"Mother how did you manage, it must have cost a fortune," her eyes clouded when her mother's hand unconsciously caressed the ringless finger. "Your ring, Mother your wedding ring, you've sold it."

"No no darling, I took one or two things to Berry's, the money was a loan." She tried to soothe her concerned daughter, "Sarah, I can redeem them any time in the next twelve months, now you stop worrying and enjoy your evening with Tom, be happy Sarah, I want everyone to know that the loveliest young woman at the celebration is my daughter."

Tom was extremely proud of his partner, he proudly introduced her to his eager colleagues, and while a succession of young men whirled her about the ballroom Sarah noted Tom danced deeply engrossed with a fair haired young woman all evening.

During a waltz an older man excused her partner, he danced perfectly but never spoke. On returning her to her seat Sarah thanked him, and was about to be seated when he bowed and said "Merci mademoiselle."

"You're a Frenchman," Sarah immediately began a conversation in his language.

The delighted man begged her to join his party on a separate table, Sarah knew Tom was longing to stay in his dance partner's company so after a brief discussion with him she accepted the Frenchman's invitation. It was when she was introduced to all heads of departments Sarah discovered Monsieur Morin had so far spent a speechless evening. He spoke no English and his counterparts were at a loss with the French language. The rest of the evening proved most enjoyable, Tom noted from time to time that Sarah's sparkling repartee was greatly admired as she acted as interpreter for the grateful Frenchman, their laughter would ring out gaily as her rusty French occasionally proved mirthful, but her quick mind soon rectified the minor faults. All too soon the evening drew to an end and Sarah left with Tom; a French business card had been accepted with the promise of a visit if she ever found herself in Paris.

On the way home she teased Tom. The red faced young man admitted he had long admired Miriam.

"Sarah she is wonderful, so clever at her job, she helped me enormously when I first joined the department." He continued shyly, "I never thought I stood a chance with her, I'm sorry for deserting you."

Sarah replied with a laugh, "Don't be silly, I know what it's like to fall for someone, just be glad she knows you exist."

"Sarah," Tom sounded shocked, "you're in love, who with? Who is he? Do I know him?"

The barrage of questions were halted as a blushing Sarah vigorously protested, "Tom you can be such a fool sometimes, stop it now and tell me about Miriam."

A reply never came as both were nearly knocked off their feet, eyes bulging in fear a terrified family came tearing out of Clare St. Sarah and Tom turned the corner to come face to face with the most heartrending scene. The women who usually sat gossiping on their steps were now running about screaming, a demented big man raised clenched fists to the heavens, his rage gave way to tears of helplessness as a police wagon disappeared around the corner. An officious body of black coated men well guarded by numerous constables marched past the horrified couple. A woman sank to her knees and pounded the pavement with her hands while letting out screams that were close to the noises of a frightened wounded animal, she raised her horror stricken face and Sarah realized the demented figure was her mother. Panic stricken steps brought Sarah to Edith's side.

"Sarah, they've taken them," Edith's horror stricken eyes almost bulged from her head.

"Who, who has taken what?" Sarah shook her mother in an effort to gain coherency.

"The children," tears tumbled in torrents down Edith's face, "the children," she sobbed, "Sarah they've taken my babies away."

Holding her mother close Sarah turned frightened enquiring eyes towards Tom, "Who are they, Tom tell me, who are those people?"

A pale-faced Tom made a helpless gesture.

"Sarah, I'm so sorry.'

"Sorry, sorry for what, we've done nothing wrong, why have they done this?" Close to tears she repeated, "Tom, please tell me, who are they, are they all policemen?"

"No," Tom shook his head, he leaned forward to help in the lifting of Edith, "they are not policemen, but they are the law, they are the nightmen, let's get your mother indoors and I'll explain."

The now unconscious Edith was put to bed by a tearful Esther. Sarah held a cool damp cloth to her mother's brow. Tom's quiet voice explained.

"Nightmen are employed by governing authorities, they swoop down on unsuspecting families, any that sleep more than two to a bed lose their children." Tom's tone became despairing, "Your mother in all innocence must have answered the questions honestly. Sarah I'm so sorry, I've never known them to raid our neighbourhood before."

"Well they have now," Sarah's voice was bitter, "Tom tell me, where do they take the children to?" As Tom shook his head she said desperately, "I must go there, I must get my brothers and sisters back, Tom they will be terrified."

"It's useless Sarah, nothing can be done tonight, you and I will go early in the morning, the appropriate local authorities will have to be found before we can even think of the children's return."

Daylight did not come soon enough for Sarah, the breaking of dawn found her hammering urgently on the O'Halleron's front door, while she and Tom sped off Edith was cared for by Esther. Wherever the couple went they were met with denials of responsibility, Sarah became more and more agitated. Pleading hysteria would not help. Tom insisted Sarah return home while he sought the advice of a friend in the police force.

Unable to assist, Jim O'Niel warned Tom he had never heard of a case where children were returned, however he was able to furnish the name of the hall where all confiscated children were assembled.

The grateful Tom sped off only to turn less enthusiastic steps towards Clare St. an hour later, he had the unenviable task of telling Sarah and Edith the children would be used to swell the English speaking Empire, the two hundred and odd children from last night's round up were already aboard a iiner heading for Canada.

Three days later Sarah sat beside her mother's bowed figure, all memories of her enjoyable evening shelved, the dress hung behind the door providing the only bit of sparkle in the room, even the eyes of the couple were dimmed with heartbreak.

A timid knock at the door revealed Kate, she placed a steaming bowl of food on the table, in a hushed voice she commiserated with the grieving mother then pleaded with Sarah to accompany her to Maggie Ellen's.

Sarah vehemently refused, until bowing to her mother's wishes she reluctantly left with Kate.

It was after Sarah had departed with Kate McKeva, Edith reached to the floor and picked up a top, she wondered where the whip which completed the toy had got to. She remembered the children's joy when Esther had appeared with a box full of her own sons out-grown treasures. Edith's gaze wandered about the room, she became tearful when the hole in the wallpaper above the bed took her attention, she remembered slapping mischievious little fingers. She drew her warm shawl closer; Esther had insisted she bought it from Berry's explaining if she didn't look after herself who would care for the children, the children, oh dear god who was looking after them now.

In an effort to escape her tormented mind Edith left the room and stood in the front door entrance. The street was unusually quiet, grieving parents went about their daily tasks forlornly, the children's voices at play were absent. Her listless steps left the house, she walked towards the Pier Head, she always felt closer to Sam near the waters, but as she came to the overhead railway she changed direction. She followed the track to the docks, her thoughts became erratic, she shouldn't have mentioned Sarah, the men need not have known of another child. She remembered Sam had told her the overhead railway structure was known locally as the docker's umbrella, if only she had been prepared, she could have said only two of children were hers, she could have told the men she was minding the other two for parents who had gone out for the evening, she could have said she herself slept in a chair.

Of no interest to boisterous dock workers the sad figure made its way to a secluded corner of Huskisson Dock. Edith looked out to sea, as tears blinded her vision she whispered "Sam, oh Sam what am I to do, this hurt inside me is unbearable," her eyes then scanned the heavens, her body shook with sobs the whisper became broken "Please dear lord forgive me, let me join my Sam."

She took a step forward, the dark murky waters greeted her greedily then swirled on having claimed yet another life.

Sarah walked confidently into Maggie Ellen's parlour, loathe to leave her mother alone she had decided Maggie Ellen's business must be dealt with speedily.

The woman sat before a roaring fire, the ever steaming kettle stood beside a warming pot, the red chenille table covering was graced with Crown Derby.

"C'mon girl," Maggie Ellen's voice was friendly "sit y'self down, Kate, scald that tea will y',"

While Kate busied herself Maggie Ellen continued "sorry t' hear about the kids girl, I'll have a word t'say t' that Lord Mayor of ours, they've never collected in my neighbourhood before, believe me they won't be back f' no more."

Sarah looked in wonderment as Kate handed her a cup of tea, she knew the crockery to be Maggie Ellen's best china, used previously for funerals and weddings only.

Kate seated herself opposite Sarah and promptly held out an eager hand towards Maggie Ellen. The now silent woman took an envelope from the folds of her dress and handed it over, Kate placed it before Sarah and pleaded "will y'read it t'us Sarah."

The unopened envelope was immediately recognized by Sarah, even now in her unhappy state over the children her heart pounded madly.

"Doesn't Maggie Ellen want to read it first." Sarah lifted Edward's letter towards his mother.

Kate answered, "Sarah, I said *will y'read it t'us*, we've had it f' a week now, please read it t' both of us."

Maggie Ellen's bowed head was scrutinised then comprehension hit Sarah suddenly, it had all been a sham, she was never given the room out of pity, the examinings of the ledger, the bandaged hand was all pretence, *Maggie Ellen could neither read nor write.* Sarah read Edward's words without concentration, when she reached the end she immediately avoided more embarrassment by re-reading it unasked.

Finally Maggie Ellen rose quietly to her feet, before leaving the room she paused to pat Sarah's shoulder in appreciation, with a resigned sigh she whispered,

"Would y' write an answer while y'here, Kate'll tell y'what t'put."

Sarah put the pen lovingly to paper, she did Kate's bidding and longed to add a few words of her own, she resisted the temptation and after completing the envelope she handed it to Kate to seal.

Arranging to call in a few days Sarah left for home, but she was to see Kate the following day when the woman ran skirts swirling on hearing of Edith's death.

Chapter 9

A taste of gracious living

Nine months later Sarah walked with Mathew in St. John's gardens, with the prized certificate recently gained, Sarah had expected signs of complete contentment from him. His quietness disturbed her, their past few evenings had ended by him begging to be allowed to ask her a question, she had so far averted the dreaded proposal, she was loathe to hurt the serious kindly young man. Since her mother's death Esther's sons had become as dearly loved brothers to her, she had accepted Miriam's suggestion of sharing a flat even though Kate and Esther had both offered her a home and the brothers had been her almost constant companions in the evenings.

Tom and Miriam were now planning to become engaged, and Sarah had eagerly accepted the council's offer of employment. The solving of the dilemma at the dance had not gone unnoticed, a repeat of the situation could now be avoided, and Sarah was more content receiving a regular salary.

Kate was visited occasionally for the reading of and replying to Edward's letters, he now seemed so far away Sarah made an effort to free her mind of him. It was after Kate had laughingly referred to Edward's earlier conquests that Sarah realised how foolish she had been, he was banished entirely from her thoughts, the correspondence became a bore and she wished he would write home less frequently.

"Sarah can I please ask you a question?" She sat forlornly on a curved concrete seat, there was no possible way of avoiding the hurt she could cause, with pain-filled eyes she faced him. "Yes Mathew, it's about time I let you get this question out of your system."

"Sarah, do you think I would make a good priest?"

"Mathew!!" Sarah was truly shocked.

"I have given quite a lot of thought to it for some time but I'm still undecided, am I good enough?"

"Mathew, oh Mathew O'Halleron I could kiss you, oh you wonderful wonderful man you would be a credit to any profession," Sarah flung her arms about the unsuspecting young man and planted a forceful kiss on his cheek.

A blushing Mathew laughed, "I didn't think it would create that much enthusiasm.

"Oh no Mathew, I wasn't giving an answer, that's something only you can decide, but please I beg you, be certain before committing yourself, as a brother I love you dearly, I want you to be happy."

He squeezed her hand in thanks for her endearing comments.

They returned to the flat in silence and over a cup of tea Mathew voiced his undecided plan to his brother, he looked shaken at Tom's forceful reply.

"No, Mathew you can't mean it, you've never shown any signs of wanting to become a priest."

"Tom, my sole aim in life is to help people."

His brother became angry. "You can do that now, look about our neighbourhood, don't you think there is more need there, priests can help spiritually, but that doesn't make life any easier for those poor people."

Mathew shook his head, "Tom, their main need is money, I haven't any."

"Then think of a way to help them, put some thought into a way to make their needs obtainable."

"That's beyond my power."

"So being a priest is going to put shoes on the children's feet, and put clothes on the people's backs, think straight Mathew. Some rich people are Catholics, what makes you think you would be put with the poor, priests go where they are sent, you could end up in some posh place where you are expected to luncheon with a squire."

Mathew showed visible signs of distress.

Sarah had heard and seen enough, "stop it, now stop it you two, this has gone far enough, you have company here in need of more lighthearted conversation."

But Tom's words hit home, not only Mathew was to reflect on his utterances.

Two weeks later Esther was buzzing around like a busy bee cooking for her sons and two guests. Sarah started the conversation, "Tom, Miriam and I were discussing your suggestions to Mathew."

"Oh I was talking out of turn, I'm sorry, but I just did not take to the idea of my brother becoming a priest."

Esther's eyebrows shot to the middle of her forehead, this was news to her, she kept her mouth closed but her ears were wide open.

Miriam spoke up "No Tom, you spoke a lot of sense, people are in need," she turned to Sarah, "you tell them what we were discussing."

All eyes turned to Sarah, she cleared her throat nervously, "we think Tom was right, someone should find a way to solve people's needs. There are a lot of young people in this area. When I lived in Clare St., my mother parted with her most treasured possessions to buy me a dress, even as poor as I was I used to long for the clothes on display in town. Well Miriam and I think someone should make it easier for young people to buy whatever clothes they want."

Mathew interrupted, "But how would they manage to pay for them."

"By instalments, they could be given an account to pay in

whatever they can afford."

Tom shook his head, "People wouldn't part with money just like that."

"Oh yes they would if the garments remained at the makers until paid for," Sarah answered.

Mathew leaned forward, his voice eager, "that would give them the incentive to work, and they would benefit more from their spare cash."

Suddenly the whole group were interested.

"We could do it, but we would need a machine and where would we find a machinist," said Mark.

"Right here," the words were spoken quietly.

They all looked in disbelief at Esther.

"I served my time as a seamstress, my mam n'dad didn't get me educated, but they wouldn't let me roam the streets, I was put t'sewing when I was twelve yr'old, but can I tell y'me most vivid memory."

Eager ears listened to her tale.

"When I was seven me and Maggie Ellen, Kate McKeva and a few others made our first holy communion. They all had snow white frocks n'veils, me mam n'dad couldn't afford t' dress me in such finery but I wasn't really bothered because the teachers told me parents I would be lent a fitting outfit. When we arrived at the church I was rushed away t' the school room next door, with me little heart bangin' in me chest I watched them open a big box."

Esther stopped and took a deep breath, it was obvious the memory was painful. Resuming she whispered "it turned out t'be the worst day of me life. When I joined the others at the altar I musta stuck out like a sore thumb, the frock they lent me was yeller with age, oh, it was lovely an clean an well pressed but I felt rotten in it. When the holy communions were finished I was rushed out and they put me own frock back on me. Walkin' home with all the others all I had t'show f' me special day was a shiny new medal hung on a ribbon round me neck."

Esther looked about her audience

"If you lot want t' help anyone, help all those little girls first, make it easier f'th' mams t'get th'r own white frocks."

Mathew's voice appealed to the others, "Let's do it, at least let's give it a try."

Tom breathed out, "It's a nice thought, it would be great if it were possible."

Mark spoke up. "How would we make ourselves known?"

Sarah smiled "I've already thought of that, I'll ask Kate to spread the word, if we succeed in this area our clothes will do the rest."

In the following weeks plans and discussions surrounded every meal, all were filled with enthusiasm. Tom and Miriam shelved their engagement plans, their savings were used to buy materials. A few empty spaces were filled on the pawnbroker's shelves and after Esther's sewing machine was brought down from the attic her parlour was turned into a work room.

Kate's assistance was invaluable; any family with six year old children were ordered to get the child up to the O'Halleron house, people were too scared to ignore her but before long a queue of eager mothers and children were to be seen happily visiting Esther's home.

Mothers were delighted, fathers were nagged into spending less money in the beer houses.

The house became so packed with completed garments Tom was forced to rent council premises, everything was moved to the nearby Norton St. As money came in it was ploughed back into the business. A big decision was made to insert six second hand sewing machines. While Esther kept the group well fed the trio's salary from the council paid the machinists wages. The group worked tirelessly without pay, Mathew and Esther devoted all their wakened time, when Mark finally left college he joined them. The orders became so vast Tom, Sarah and Miriam decided to give up their council employment; this decision was reached after all the work-force attended the next holy communion procession in Holy Cross church, they knew they had succeeded when Esther looked at the equally dressed children tearfully, a sense of achievement filled the whole group as the procession of miniature brides and frill shirted seven year olds beamed with joy on this their special day.

Tom took charge of finance, Miriam headed a customer's measurements and fittings department, Mark was the stock-keeper and Mathew was a general dogsbody, he was willing to help wherever needed. Esther had been released from factory duty and was more than pleased to provide meals in her own kitchen for the heads of the firm.

Sarah was their buyer, she travelled to the mills choosing cloth, she was the team's representative and her firm business tactics earned the company the deepest of respect. Times had brought about a dramatic change in lifestyle.

A taste of gracious living came to Sarah through Desmond Tyler. On her second visit to the mill she became conscious of the tall fair-haired man's silent observation, she smiled and bade him good morning before returning her attention to the stockman who informed her the material she required was out of stock. Sarah's crestfallen look jolted the observer into action, "I will attend to Miss, Miss?" He glanced quickly at the order sheet, and continued with a smile "Miss Swanson myself." The stockman looked surprised before retreating to the factory. "Thank you," Sarah smiled pleasantly, she extended her hand while enquiring, "and you are?"

"Desmond Tyler."

"The mill owner?" Sarah sounded surprised.

"No, I'm the manager, son of the mill owner."

Sarah's cheeks pinked prettily as he held onto her hand,

"I'm sorry," he gave an embarrassed laugh as he hastily loosened the hold. He drew the cloth pattern book towards him.

"Which did you order?"

"Your stockman said it was unavailable."

Desmond drew a gold watch from his waistcoat pocket, then without a sign of his normal shyness he said,

"If I magic up your order will you return the favour?"

Sarah was taken back, she looked at him with uncertainty.

"Oh, only lunch," he was quick to put her at ease. "Look you have to eat and so do I, there's quite a good place nearby." They both smiled as Sarah nodded her assent, "yes, thank you Mr. Tyler, that would be very nice."

"Desmond, please call me Desmond."

"In that case I am Sarah, you must call me Sarah."

That lunch led to many more outings, it became a habit for Sarah to stay the night at his parent's home. Her orders were given top priority, and her place in the world of fashion was confirmed by the people she delighted at dinner parties. It was no surprise to her partners when she kept returning with yet more orders, she was the main source for all the outside interest which helped swell the company's workload.

Sarah would laugh at Desmond's petulance, he objected to his parent's manipulating her time. The delighted mill owners had increased the number of social evenings their son had always backed out of in the past, Sarah was hugged and kissed like a long lost daughter whenever she appeared, in fact the servants were no longer told to air the guest room, it was now known as Miss Sarah's room. Sarah loved every minute of her visits, Desmond's friendship and his parent's down to earth approach filled her with warmth, evenings spent in the surrounding countryside brought back happy memories of her childhood.

Desmond reminded her in many ways of her father, his ready laughter once the shyness barrier was broken, his delight in keeping the destination of their outing secret, his affection towards off duty weavers; they were hailed by families wherever they went. She told him of her family, not in a mournful way, she spoke of their happier times.

The smartly dressed young woman stepped from the taxi, before ascending the steps she paused and looked up to the first floor windows, a porter came to her side, "can I be of assistance Madam?"

Her large amber eyes noted Jevons had been replaced by a younger man.

"No thank you, I am to join Mr. O'Halleron's party, I can

find my own way."

She entered the hotel and without the hesitation of a stranger she walked confidently to the lounge. Tom rose to meet her, she was the last to arrive. The long day at the mills had prevented Sarah from questioning him, his message had been passed on by a hastily retreating Miriam that morning. "Tom what on earth are you up to? All this grandeur means something's in the air," she smiled her greetings to the rest of the company. Tom nodded to a hovering head waiter.

"Our table is waiting, Miriam and I have news for you all but it will have to wait until after dinner."

As they entered the dining room Sarah was pleased to see the seatings had been re-arranged, the space where she had sat as a child was taken by a beef-carving chef. The company were so obviously happy she had dreaded facing memories, but she need not have worried for she found comfort in remembering her mother as the attractive lady who had enhanced these surroundings. Horrendous imaginings of her father drowning were replaced by memories of a tall handsome much alive laughing man striding about the hotel.

The meal was a happy occasion, Esther fondly rebuked Mark for eating greedily, happy chatter and laughter invaded the normally sedate setting. Coffee had just been served when Tom took Miriam's hand in his, in answer to his enquiring look she nodded happily. He gave a slight cough then announced,

"Miriam and I have decided on the date for our marriage," he gave his fiancée a loving look, "I still can't believe my luck but this lovely lady has consented to be my wife in six months."

While the rest of the company rejoiced at the news, Mark the jester gave a forced sigh of relief, "Oh is that all, I thought for a moment I was being given the push and this was my farewell do."

Amid laughter the happy couple were congratulated, the conversation turned to clothes and bridal gowns.

Esther looked on fondly, "I am so proud of y'all, while helping others y've all done well f'y'selves,"

"We could never have done it without your help mother,"

Mathew kissed her cheek, "the firm is going from strength to strength."

"Perhaps so Mathew but we need new designs," everyone showed interest when Sarah aired her views. "Haven't you noticed, all the maker's are using the same designs? People's clothes are becoming like uniforms, we need our own designer, someone with fresh ideas from outside Liverpool."

"Yes, yes," Tom was enthusiastic.

The conversation was still in progress back at Esther's house, the final decisions found Sarah and Mathew were to travel to London in search of new ideas, the evening came to a happy conclusion.

On her next visit to the mill Sarah told Desmond of her plans and promised to see him on her return.

Two weeks later the pair travelled south, their first day was spent getting their bearings. Sarah loved Buckingham Palace but Mathew was devoid of enthusiasm, he had been reared within the shadows of the finest architecture. He was critical of the southern offerings, if the truth be known he was already homesick. Although they were met with helpful kindness Mathew hankered to get back to his beloved city, that is until the day he was introduced to Y'vette. Sarah looked on with amusement at his fuddled manner whenever the young French designer appeared. The twosome soon became a threesome being wined and dined by southerners seeking northern business.

Y'vette was a well sought after trade asset, she was in the position to have many doors opened and she made sure the couple met all the right people. While Mathew was besotted, Sarah's quick eyes took in all the trade advancements. Though she received quite a few compliments she made it clear her visit was purely a business venture, but one eager person's pleadings were rewarded with a few dinner dates so Sarah would not feel she was playing gooseberry to the now romantic Mathew and Y'vette, but when an ecstatic Mathew told her of his and Y'vette's intended visit to France she joined them eagerly. France was the fashion house of the world, she couldn't wait to see the modern designs first hand. Before leaving London she ordered the most up to date machinery, including a felling and overlocking machine. She was spurred with enthusiasm and toured the French fashion houses with unflagging energy. Outwardly she was a cool business woman but inside she rejoiced in this Aladdin's cave, even Mathew's news of his intended whirlwind marriage didn't reach the same height of happy delirium.

Mathew was well received by Y'vette's family and friends, everyone admired her choice of this shy Englishman. When the couple made known their intention of returning to Liverpool together Y'vette's parents insisted on a quick French wedding ceremony.

Sarah found herself bridesmaid at her beloved Mathew's wedding. The solemn vows were doubly enjoyed as they were taken twice in the French tradition. The outdoor festivities brought back old memories of her first evening in Gerard St., everyone seemed to turn up to toast the happy couple. It was when Mathew and his bride took to the makeshift courtyard dance floor that a hand touched Sarah's elbow, a Frenchman requested a dance. He had only taken a few steps when Sarah exclaimed, "Monsieur Morin is it really you?"

A beaming smile answered her question, the dance was forgotten, a great deal of cheek kissing and hugs were witnessed by his smiling family, amid a babble of excitement she was introduced by her delighted partner.

Later in the evening Sarah learned of Monsieur Morin's distress, he and his wife feared for their daughter; Estelle, the eighteen year old mademoiselle was determined to take her designer enthusiasm to London. Sarah eased their minds by suggesting the girl joined her in Liverpool. The grateful parents were relieved to see the interest shown by their youngster, and quickly gave their consent. So arriving back in Liverpool the returning group were swelled to four.

Esther cried with joy on meeting her daughter-in-law, she was so conscious of the shabbyness of her surrounding neighbourhood she had demanded Tom book a hotel room for the bridal couple. With great relief she found her worry was unnecessary, Y'vette was blind to all except her adoring husband.

Tom was delighted, "you wily old fox, what happened to all the talk of celibacy? Your the one that wanted to join the priesthood, and not only do you return a married man you have two modern designers in tow," the two brothers hugged each other affectionately.

Mark was conspicious in his silence, his shyness on meeting Estelle was amazing, the nudging and winks from his brothers brought a furious blushing to his face, his jesting nature was stilled. Miriam was ecstatic, Sarah had presented her with a full roll of fine french lace. The next couple of months found the most exquisite wedding gown taking shape; the whole group were in a state of excitement over the forthcoming wedding, four machinists were separated from the rest of the workforce and put to the creating of perfection under the skilful guidance of the two french girls.

Chapter 10

The bronzed handsome figure

A week before the wedding Sarah spent the night at Esthers, with the need to catch an early morning train to the mills Esther's house was more convenient, she spent an enjoyable evening listening to the older woman reminiscing and catching up on local gossip. Esther looked at the tall attractive girl sitting before her, she took in the expertly bobbed hairstyle, its lustre had returned and shone in the firelight, the smartness of clothing, and the petiteness of the sensible shoes.

"Your mother would be proud of y' Sarah."

In the stillness of the room Sarah smiled tenderly

"If only she had waited a few more years, oh Esther I could have made her happy."

"She's happy now girl, she's where she wanted t'be, with y'dad."

"Yes, I think you are right, but one day I will travel to Canada and find my brothers and sisters, I don't care how long it takes I will find them."

"I pray's t'God y'will love, y'deserve some happiness f'all y'done f'people."

Sarah came alive, her eyes sparkled. "They look better don't they Esther? Have you ever seen so many of them employed? This district supplied most of our workforce, they want to work Esther, they actually want to work."

"Lord love y' Sarah they owe y' a lot, Even Kate sings y' praises, she doesn't have t' bully anyone anymore they all go f'y' new styles of th' own accord."

"How is Kate, Esther? It's so long since I last saw her, I've been so busy."

"I know love, I know y'have, an Kate understands too, she's fine, always asks about y', but poor Maggie Ellen's not well at all, she caught her hand on a rusty nail when they was rent collectin' in Circus St. one day an she's never set foot outside her house since."

"I must make an effort to visit sometime next week. Tell Kate if you see her, I will be away for four days."

"You'll be too busy with our Tom's weddin' when y'get back I'll tell her t'expect y'in about ten days."

"Yes, yes that's fine, thank you, now then if I don't get to bed I'll never catch that train." Sarah had enjoyed the evening and went happily off to bed.

The following day she invited Desmond to the wedding, to her disappointment he told her remorsefully he was unable to back out of a previously arranged commitment.

A week later she was in the flat amid a flurry of excitement, Y'vette and Estelle had worked miracles, not only had they created the most wonderful wedding gown, they had designed the most daring of bridesmaid dresses for themselves and Sarah. When the sheer slipper satin slid onto her body to reveal bare shoulders Sarah thought this was the closest she had come to looking as striking as the Steble fountain ladies.

The service was beautiful, the church of Holy Cross was packed to capacity, everyone seemed to want to see Tom's wedding. Sarah noticed Kate in the crowd at the rear and smiled happily, but later when she looked for the tall figure Kate had gone.

The reception was held at the Adelphi and Sarah sat beside a tearful Esther.

"Oh Sarah, I can't tell y'how happy I am, wasn't the service lovely, an you girls an my lads look beautiful," she broke down crying and repeated "I can't tell y'how happy I am."

Sarah laughed, "Well no-one would guess it, wipe your eyes, you now have the daughter you always wanted."

"Oh I already had that in you love," Esther smiled through her tears, "but one more is welcome."

"Esther you're a love, now tell me, did you see Kate at the church? When I went to speak to her she'd gone."

Esther became solemn, "I have something t' tell y' Sarah, Maggie Ellen died that night y'slept in my house, it's been kept from y' in case y' got upset, we knew y' was lookin forward t'th wedding an we didn't want t'spoil it f'y. She got poison in that bad hand an nothin' could be done f'her, she had a good life girl, poor Kate'll miss her more than anyone."

"Oh Kate, Kate," Sarah looked troubled, "Esther I love that woman I hope she isn't grieving too much."

"She loves you as well, it was her as put us up t'not tellin' y', be happy t'night Sarah then y'can go n'see her tomorrow, she understands."

Tom halted their conversation, he was happy.

"Give your big brother a kiss on his wedding day," he playfully planted a kiss on Sarah's cheek, he felt her stiffen in his arms and looked in alarm at the pallor of her face, he followed her gaze and saw his friend Edward had arrived. Sarah lifted her long dress and fled the room.

"Sarah, Sarah," when Tom caught up with her in the foyer she was panic stricken. He swept her high in the air and whirled her about as he laughed, "It's him isn't it, I've always wondered what chump left you loving him so much."

"Tom please let me go, I want to go home."

She was ready to flee when a voice behind her said,

"There you are Tom, I thought I'd joined the wrong reception."

"No Edward, nice to see you again."

While the two men shook hands Sarah went weak kneed looking at the tall bronzed handsome man. If it were possible he was even better looking than she remembered, his eyes were bluer, his chin firmer, she thought helplessly, he is perfect.

Tom encircled her waist with a supportive arm.

"Have you met Sarah?"

Edward shook his head and smiled as he held out his hand once again. Sarah thought she was about to faint when he clapsed her hand in his, she felt Tom's arm tighten as he gave Edward a friendly warning.

"Sarah is wonderful, she is my adopted sister, if you like what you see Edward be warned, she's not to be treated like the girls in the neighbourhood."

Edward put on a mock hurt expression while Sarah blushed furiously.

"Will your wonderful sister dance with me? And Tom as you seem to be bossing this party will you order her to look after me? I'm a stranger here now."

Tom laughed and put Sarah in Edward's charge. As they walked back to the ballroom he whispered "be happy little sister."

Sarah was strangely affected by Tom's remark about neighbourhood girls, she had a pretty shrewd idea of the meaning and pulled herself together. She also remembered Kate's joking revelations so she treated Edward as she would any other wedding guest, never once did she show her true feelings as they danced the evening away. She calmly pointed out different couples and explained who they were, she spoke of London and went into raptures over the French wedding, she desperately hoped she seemed outwardly calm. Edward was deeply engrossed, he listened to her talk of the mills and the fashion business, her lively chatter helped ease the sadness of his recent bereavement.

When the celebration ended she allowed Edward to see her home. As it was a fine evening they walked; on the way she confided her longing to find her brothers and sisters, but when they arrived at their destination she hastily bade him goodnight and fled indoors. The deserted Edward stood for awhile in shocked surprise, he wondered what he had done to frighten her away, she had certainly not given any sign of rejecting his company throughout the evening, he looked up at the more recent of lit windows and became thoughtful, a few giggling females who had been ogling the bronzed handsome figure went unnoticed as he turned his steps towards home.

Although the following day was a Sunday it was not a day of rest for Sarah, Estelle and Mark. It had been decided that Tom and Miriam would set up temporary home at the flat on their return. The three made an early start at clearing the place in readiness for Monday morning decorators. The two girls had given way to Esther's pleadings and were to move into her home until the bridal couple found a permanent place to live. While a week's honeymoon was spent in the Isle of Man a rota was kept up on checks of the decorating. On Sarah's visit the workmen told her of a foreigner who had been seen watching the premises. Sarah brushed aside their warnings as there was more than one flat in the house.

It was at Esther's house while all were rejoicing in the return of the newlyweds that Mark and Estelle sprang their surprise, a table had been booked for ten at the small but friendly St. George Hotel on Lime Street. The blushing couple told the delighted group they preferred the less formal surroundings to celebrate their engagement. Sarah was pleased to hear Monsieur Morin would be present, but was thrown into a panic when she realised she had only two weeks to find an escort.

The following day with her own work schedule to catch up with she paid Desmond a visit, he greeted her affectionately and once her business was attended to took her to lunch. After explaining her problem he readily agreed to attend the engagement party. It was a relieved Sarah who regretfully took her leave of him to race off to her other commitments.

News awaited Sarah when she arrived home, it was as she eased her tired body into a comfortable armchair that Tom again insisted she needed an assistant.

"Yes Tom" she readily agreed, "but where do we find one."

"I already have," Tom sounded triumphant.

Tiredness was suddenly secondary, Sarah showed keen interest.

"Who Tom, who have you found?"

"The sister of a chap I went to school with, she's a gem. Sarah you'll like her, she's educated, she speaks three languages and she's bored stiff with what she's doing now."

"Good, when can I meet her," Sarah was eager.

"Tomorrow. If you accept her Sarah she's willing to start immediately."

"Y'need some help, y'can't go on killin y'self forever," 'bout time y'took a holiday." Esther spoke from the depths of an opposite armchair, the others nodded their agreement.

Sarah laughed, "Thank you all for thinking I have one foot in the grave," she waved aside their protests, "I'm only joking, I admit we do need someone, I may be missing out on a lot of business because I don't have the time to stop look and listen." She stretched her arms before saying to no-one in particular, "Lord I'm tired, isn't it peculiar the more money you acquire the harder you have to work."

"Well after tomorrow you can ease off, we can afford an extra pair of hands," Tom threw up his arms, "we can afford ten pairs if it means you would enjoy life more."

"Thank you Tom, one pair is quite sufficient, I am looking forward to meeting your friend's sister. What's her name?"

"Cathrine O'Niel," Tom's voice became reassuring, "you will like her Sarah."

"That's enough talk of work," Esther rose to her feet,

"Tom you an Y'vette might as well have y'evenin meal here, I've cooked plenty so sit y'selves at th'table." As she disappeared into the kitchen she called "I saw Kate McKeva today Sarah, she sez if y' has time this evenin' she would like t'see y'."

Sarah's heart suddenly raced, she had put off the longed for visit because of Edward's presence in the house. After dinner it was unsure steps that took her to Gerard St.

Kate beamed her welcome, she ushered Sarah into the less formal rear room, a bright fire crackled in the grate, tea was made from an already steaming kettle.

While Kate fussed, Sarah strained her ears for sounds of other activity within the house.

"Sit down Sarah, y'don't have t'wait t'be asked in this house, y'know y'always welcome. Oh wait a minute, let's move that first." Kate removed a silk nightdress which lay crumpled on the chair she had indicated, her voice became vexed.

"That Lilli is so untidy, I f'one will be glad t'see th' back of her, she leaves th' bedroom in a terrible mess, powder all over th' place, thank's be t'God Edward gets her out of here every evenin." Kate did not notice Sarah's sudden tension and babbled on "I sometimes think people are goin crackers, she was named after some woman who sang on th' music halls."

"Kate," Sarah sounded agitated, "I'm sorry but I will have to leave after the tea, I hope you understand I have to be up early tomorrow."

After spending only fifteen minutes in Kate's company she made a hasty retreat. She drew into the shadows as a taxi came down Gerard St., and watched as it drew to a stop outside the house she had just left. Her heart sank as she recognised the tall figure that gallantly helped a beautiful blonde alight, she stood motionless until they disappeared indoors. Feelings of misery overcame Sarah as she returned to Esther's.

Cathrine O'Niel was a very striking woman. When her tall sophisticated figure entered the factory office Sarah took to the dark haired person immediately, the slim body was held straight, her walk self assured, the expertly trimmed hair curled naturally about her face. Sarah noted the minimum of discreetly placed cosmetics, the fingernails were manicured to perfection, each one revealed a perfectly shaped half-moon. Sarah's mind was racing, this is what the firm needed. The form before her suddenly became an imaginary clothes horse, in the short distance between the door and the desk Sarah had mentally dressed the figure in half a dozen different outfits. The young woman's personality proved as dynamic as her appearance, she was not only to halve Sarah's workload she became a treasured friend to the whole group, so much so that when they insisted she join the engagement celebration she readily agreed and requested her brother should be allowed to escort her. The restaurant booking was increased to twelve.

Sarah enjoyed Cathrine's company the first week, the pair turned many heads as the newcomer was taught the trade. Sarah kept their visits to the more local of calls to start Cathrine's fashion career. The work became less arduous as they breezed through the weeks itinerary. It was on the next Monday lunch time that all were amazed to discover a very different Sarah.

The two were laughing as they made their way to the factory office, Cathrine continued ahead as Mark halted Sarah with a query. Sarah reached the door in time to hear Cathrine's velvet tones exclaim "Edward, oh my dear how lovely to see you, I heard you were home." She embraced the smiling Edward saying, "how many hearts did you break in Egypt?"

He did not answer, his eyes were riveted on Sarah, she stood still in the doorway feeling amazed, she thought angrily, did this man know everyone in Liverpool?

"Oh there you are," Tom sounded cheerful, "Sarah we were just making arrangements for this evening. Will you take pity on Edward and make up the number for a visit to the theatre?"

Sarah's face turned an angry crimson, "Tom how dare you, I'm sure Mr. Murray is not short of any number of partners, I object to being treated like a spare part, in future you will run your own life and kindly leave me to run mine."

Before turning on her heel she told her open-mouthed audience she would take the rest of the day off, she added scathingly "To look after my own business."

Sarah fled to Esther, loathe to explain her distress she sobbed out her intention of taking a few days holiday, within an hour she was aboard a train heading towards Desmond.

Desmond was kindness itself, her sudden unscheduled appearance alarmed him. On sighting her he reached for his jacket and shepherded her out of the mill, they were well into the country when he drew the car to a halt. Sarah allowed a sudden rush of scalding tears to run unchecked down her face. "Sarah, Sarah, what is it?" Desmond's voice was tender, he continued as he enfolded her sobbing body in his arms, "who has the power to hurt you so much?"

Without answering she took comfort in his embrace. They stayed this way for a while without speaking, until eventually she struggled for composure.

"I won't burden you with my troubles Desmond, let me sort myself out first," she turned appealing eyes towards him. "Will your parents mind my company for a few days? Will it be convenient?"

Desmond laughed, "you silly goose, you know you are always welcome. Come on I'll take you there now, it will surprise you how comforting a change can be, from now on things can only get better."

Sarah threw him a grateful look for not prying.

Mr. and Mrs. Tyler greeted her warmly. Sarah was immediately ordered upstairs by Desmond, he waited until she was out of earshot before warning his parents against planning vigorous social events, he made the excuse Sarah was a little off colour and had come to them for a rest. His concerned parents readily agreed and afforded Sarah the most peaceful of comfort.

The next four days were spent in the tranquility of the countryside, although Sarah still hurt inside she felt her problem was a million miles away. Then Desmond quietly reminded her of Mark's engagement, he waited until they were alone one evening in the comfort of his parents' lounge, he handed her a glass of sherry, "Sarah I have something to say." She looked up at him dreading a confrontation.

"Desmond please."

"No my dear, you can't keep hiding your head in the sand, if you have a problem let me try to help. Sarah I always felt there was someone, I had an agonizing time stopping myself from falling in love with you, you have grown more dear to me with every passing day, but I always knew I was not the one you wanted."

"Oh Desmond," her voice was a whisper, "I love you so very much, just as I love Mark, Mathew and Tom, you all mean so very much to me."

"But not as much as your mystery man. Now I'll tell you what we will do," his voice took on a lighter tone, "you and I Miss are going to put on our glad rags and knock them all dead in Liverpool."

With tear-filled eyes Sarah nodded her agreement.

Chapter 11

Oh, Mary Ann

Sarah was embarrassed by the jubilation on her return. While Desmond sat looking out of place in Esther's parlour she was surrounded by her recently worried friends. Amid all the greetings her eyes met Tom's, he blinked furiously as he whispered "I'm sorry Sarah."

"Come here," her arms encircled his shoulders, then as he hugged her close her whisper came brokenly, "forgive me, please Tom forgive me."

It was only after the surreptitious use of his handkerchief that Tom's voice rang out, "Come on you lot, let's paint the town red."

On leaving the house Desmond jokingly demanded his rights as escort, for the cheerful company of men jostled for position next to Sarah. Amid happy laughter Monsieur Morin was heard to call out, "I claim the first dance Sarah, you and I will show everyone how it should be done." He took the following chiding remarks in good spirit.

The arrangements at the restaurant were superb, while normal business carried on as usual the engagement party's table had been prepared at the far end of the room. Before being seated Tom introduced Cathrine to Desmond and Sarah to Jim O'Niel, the foursome were positioned next to each other at the table. Amid all the frivolity Sarah was amused to spot Desmond eyeing Cathrine, the couple appeared to be mutually attracted, she gained Desmond's attention by tugging at his sleeve, as he met her sly grin he blushed furiously.

"Sarah, she's absolutely wonderful," he whispered, "do you think she will agree to see me again?"

Sarah giggled and leaned in front of him, "Cathrine, would you mind changing seats with me? I want a word in your brother's ear." She stood up without waiting for a reply, then when Cathrine moved she sat herself down between Desmond and Jim.

"You don't remember me do you?"

Jim looked at the lovely young woman, he shook his head in puzzlement.

"Do you remember the florist losing her purse?"

He thought back and nodded, "Yes, yes Mrs. Reilly." Then recognition flooded his eyes, "you're never that Sarah?"

She nooded happily.

He took hold of her hand, "Well I never, do you know love I have often wondered what happened to you, that was my first case, I'm with the C.I.D. now, I'm so pleased to see you have done so well," he broke off suddenly. "Oh there he is," Jim turned to Sarah apologetically, "excuse me a moment Sarah, I told my friend I would be spending the evening here, he has been wanting to see me about something or other, I'll be back soon, now don't go away."

As he rose Sarah smiled, but it froze on her face as she saw his friend was Edward. A hand covered hers beneath the table and held on firmly. Desmond had followed her eyes and looked at the newcomer with interest. Sarah felt sick when she saw the beautiful Lilli, Edward's companion was exquisite, she was so tiny, every inch of her was perfection. Her skin was like that of a china doll, the enormous blue eyes seemed to cover half her face, the couple were both better looking than any moving picture stars.

"Steady darling, you have done so well up to now," Desmond was whispering, "don't spoil it now."

Sarah clung onto his hand as Edward's eyes met hers, his look became suddenly stony and he immediately turned his back towards her, she felt she was in a dream world. Jim was writing something on a piece of paper, he tucked it into his pocket, then he rose to his feet and shook hands, he returned to Sarah's side as the couple left.

Neither Cathrine or Miriam seemed to mind when Desmond and Tom suddenly paid all their attention to Sarah, and although she seemed to enjoy herself her laugh was a pitch higher than normal. The evening seemed never ending to her, grief and longing tore at her heart.

The following two weeks found Sarah working like a beaver, she threw herself whole heartedly into her work, only once did she allow herself to think of Edward. She regretted her outburst before him but then decided to put the whole mess behind her, he would probably marry Lilli, and there was little use in pining for him. She was pleased Desmond and Cathrine had found each other, that Tom and Miriam were happy and Mathew and Y'vette were still blissful. She smiled at the thought of Mark, his nature had changed so much he was no longer the jester, his caring ways delighted the young Estelle. Estelle's whole family were expected for the wedding, the couple were to be married at Holy Cross in three months time.

Sarah sighed, all this wonderful romance surrounded her but it was not meant to happen for her. She supposed she should be grateful God had given her the sense to earn money to seek out her brothers and sisters. She wondered what they were like now, were they happy, would she recognize them? She was pleased Cathrine had joined the firm, she would probably marry Desmond but in the meantime she was a godsend. Sarah's sudden decision to take a holiday had received everyone's blessing.

Sarah kept a low profile the few weeks before leaving, her heart ached so much she thought it would break if she were to see Edward and Lilli together again. She made up her mind to use this trip to forget him, it would be a case of having to for she firmly believed the couple would be married before her return. That was why it had been a relief when the others had agreed to allow her four weeks holiday. It wasn't as if she were letting them down, Christine was competent, she had more than proved Tom's expectations, and it was the first time she had taken time off, even the evenings spent with Desmond and his family were followed by early morning visits elsewhere. She would miss them all but this trip had been her sole reason for continuing work after the firm became established. It had been the morning after Mark and Estelle's engagement that Sarah had entered the travel agents in Water Street and booked a passage to Canada, the others had been surprised but they wished her luck in her mission. Esther had wept but had dried her tears when Sarah promised to return in four weeks with or without her brothers and sisters.

The crossing was pleasant, but Sarah did not waste her time on board, instead of relaxing she questioned the crew from the captain down to the lowliest of crew. She gained little information about the confiscated children, all the crews' tales were similar; the youngsters were afraid and fretful but as they neared the end of the trip more smiles were to be seen, their routine was strict but they were well cared for, names were forgotten, there were so many of them but one thing was made clear to Sarah, not one grown up on those trips enjoyed or agreed with what was happening and were grateful they were not expected to experience it often.

Sarah had no idea where to start on her arrival, the ship's captain had advised her to have a word with the dock authorities. Having settled in a hotel it took three days for Sarah to gain a meeting with an official. The man blustered on hearing her business and advised her to contact higher representatives of the Government.

It was a fellow traveller who led Sarah on a hopeful path. Feeling dejected and miserable in a strange land Sarah had returned to the hotel, while at dinner another guest commented on the happenings at the docks a few years ago. Part of her luggage had gone missing on a previous trip, she was summoned to the baggage department to file a report. While there she witnessed a most harrowing sight, thousands of children lined the docks, some were little more than babies, they were made to enter a large communal hall, her mind had never known peace since.

After dinner the woman was singled out, and begging her pardon Sarah beseeched her for more information. On hearing the whole sorry tale the traveller took Sarah in a taxi and revealed the whereabouts of the hall, she regretted being unable to help further.

The following day found Sarah banging on the locked hall door, the place was little more than a huge dock shed.

"No use knocking there Marm, the office is across the dock road."

Sarah eyed the speaker, she was a bonny teenager, the sun had bleached her hair almost white. Earnest blue eyes took in Sarah's well dressed figure.

"Can you show me where please?"

"Of course I can, I work there," the girl spoke with a rich Canadian accent. The pair fell in step.

"Your English aren't you?" The girl sounded inquisitive.

"Yes, yes I am."

"Where did you come from? London?"

"No, I came from Liverpool."

Arrival at the office halted the questioning, a handsome young man rose to meet Sarah, "I'm Joshua Clarke," as he shook hands Sarah introduced herself. On hearing of the reason for her presence in Canada he promised to help as much as possible. His friendliness helped relax Sarah.

"Sit down and I'll take some details,"

Sarah hoped this muscular blonde haired man could at least set her in the right direction.

"Now, how many brothers and sisters are there?"

"Two sisters, two brothers."

"And their names?"
"Mary Ann, Agnes, Alexander and Robert Swanson."

"Why does one of them have two names?" It was the girl who spoke.

"Ruthie please, Miss Swanson is here on business."

Joshua looked apologetic.

"No it's alright," Sarah smiled and turned towards the girl. "When I was christened my father wanted me to have his mother's name, but his mother insisted she would rather me have her mother's name, so I was named Sarah after my great grandmother. When my sister came along she was named after both grandmothers, Mary after my mother's mother and Ann after my father's mother, she was always referred to by both names out of respect for both grandmothers."

"English people are not so nice are they?"

"Ruthie," Joshua sounded angry, "how dare you."

"Well, they have kids and let them be sent away, then when the kids are grown up they come here all horrified. No need to look like that," her insolent look met Sarah's worried face, "we're not cannibals, we don't eat them on their arrival". Then defiantly, "When I have kids no-one but me will rear them."

"*Ruth*, please Miss Swanson, accept my apologies, I will do what I can this afternoon and contact you this evening at your hotel, meanwhile I will have a few words with this youngster here."

Sarah took her leave, she felt angry at the girl's outspoken manner, had Ruth been a little older she would have received a fitting answer.

Later that day Joshua arrived at the hotel. Sarah had calmed herself and met him eagerly, "have you any news Mr. Clarke?"

He smiled and led her to a seat in the lounge, "I'm fully aware of the urgency but slow down, you can't expect success in one afternoon."

"But I'm here for such a short time, I've used up four days already."

"Yes I know, now look," Joshua leaned forward and took both her hands in his, "don't get upset by what I'm about to tell you." Panic spread across Sarah's face.

"No, no, nothing wrong," he was quick to assure her, "it's just that it's the weekend, I won't be able to resume investigating until Monday, but in the meantime you can fill me in with more details."

Sarah looked disappointed but she nodded, "such as?"

"Ages, you didn't tell me the children's ages or the date they sailed, it would be a great help if you could give the name of the ship that brought them here."

At Sarah's crestfallen look he quickly continued "no matter, just their ages will do," he tried to put her at ease by smiling.

"Could be kids with the same names, you don't want to come all this way to meet someone elses kids."

"Thank you Mr. Clarke, thank you for all you are doing, I don't know what I'd have done without your help."

"Well I've done little so far but I will, I promise, now tell me, do you intend sitting about this place all weekend waiting for Monday?"

"I'll find a book to read."

"No, absolutely no, you can't go home and say you didn't visit Niagara Falls. I'm spending my weekend there, come with me."

Sarah laughed at his forward manner then shrugged "Yes Mr. Clarke, I would like that very much if you're sure I'm not a bother."

"Well you will be if you keep calling me Mr. Clarke, from now on I'm Josh and you're Sarah, okay?"

Sarah smiled and agreed.

The weekend was thoroughly enjoyed, Josh had booked rooms at a hotel and both found pleasure in viewing the magnificent Falls. Even though they were supplied with oil skins Sarah felt chilly, she started to shiver and Josh hugged her close. Sarah attempted to laugh but was unable to stop her teeth chattering. "There's only one cure for that," he raised her chin with one finger and looked into her eyes, then he brought his lips down towards hers. She lowered her head and buried her face in his chest and they stood close until he called out gaily, "Come on Miss, a hot drink is what you need."

After dinner they strolled in the hotel gardens. Josh had been subdued throughout the meal, "Sarah, I'm sorry if I offended you today."

Sarah blushed and said lamely, "you didn't offend me, you must save your kisses for someone special. I haven't done anything to merit that attention, but," she became mischievious "you have," she laughed aloud and put both hands to his face, she drew his mouth down to hers and kissed him.

With a sigh of relief he cradled her in his arms, "Sarah" he whispered "you are beautiful, but I get the message." He looked into her eyes, "I rushed it didn't I? But we'll be good friends won't we?"

Sarah kissed his cheek lightly and made no attempt to move from his embrace, she laid her head on his shoulder and whispered "Yes Josh, I hope so."

Monday came and Sarah hung about the hotel waiting for a call, Josh left a message to say he would meet her early that evening. All keyed up Sarah ran towards him as he strode through the hotel reception.

"Have you any news?" she could tell by his laughing eyes he had, she pleaded happily, "tell me, oh Josh where are they? Tell me."

"Hold on Sarah, let's sit down first."

She raced to the lounge and sat on a settee, reaching out to him she pulled him down beside her clasping his hand tightly, "where are they?" she whispered.

"In the country on a farm."

"Can we get there now? Oh Josh please say yes."

"Sarah you must calm down, we have to be very sure first."

Fighting to control her emotions she sat quiet.

"How many years is it since you've seen them?"

"Six years."

"And how old was the youngest one then?"

"Robert, he was three."

"That would make him nine now," Josh gave a satisfied smile

then continued "I think I have located him, and maybe Mary Ann, but Sarah I must warn you there's no details of the other two, I'll keep trying but so far I've drawn a blank."

"Josh you're wonderful, oh I could kiss you."

Josh laughed "be my guest anytime it suits you."

Sarah hugged him.

"Alright now look, I'm calm, I'm not rushing you, but Josh please when can I see them?"

"The day after tomorrow, I will have to get in touch with the farm people tomorrow and I'll do my best to make arrangements for a visit the next day,"

"A visit, but I've come to take them home."

"Okay, okay, let's see what happens, I'll come with you," his eyes twinkled, as he added "and Sarah."

She looked at him hopefully.

"They have a child called Mary,"

"Wonderful, oh Josh how can I thank you, perhaps Mary Ann will know where the other two are."

Rachel Cameron was a pleasant woman who greeted the visitor's warmly, Sarah judged the fair haired woman's age around fortyish. Although made welcome Sarah was conscious of the fearful looks which occasionally replaced Rachel's smile, it was after Josh's introduction the woman first spoke to Sarah,

"Am I to understand you are my son's sister?"

Sarah felt a surge of unease, the woman's voice was slightly defiant stressing the *my*.

"Robert's sister, yes I am, please may I see him now?"

"At the moment he is helping his father, they will be here shortly, but first Miss Swanson may I ask the meaning of your visit." The woman's calm voice suddenly changed as she rushed on, "please," pleading eyes met Sarah's, "he has settled, he remembers nothing of his English life, his only memory is of being on a big ship."

"Hello there, see you managed to find our place alright."

Andrew Cameron strode towards them, he held out a friendly hand to Sarah, he looked at his wife, "a long cool drink wouldn't go amiss dear." His wife disappeared into the house as he lowered his tall body into a veranda seat, he directed his next words to Sarah "Rachel is upset, she thinks you are going to take our son, will you stay with us for a few days, you must realise you are a stranger to Robert."

"Where is he, please may I see him now?" Sarah ignored the invitation.

"Robert, come here son," the man's loud call brought a boy hurrying from the rear of the building. He was a healthy looking nine year old, he threw an inquisitive look towards the visitors then halted before Andrew.

"Yes pa."

"I want to introduce our visitors, this is Mr. Joshua Clarke." Sarah watched as the boy shook hands with Josh, she wondered why she had not been introduced first then she understood when the man's voice continued slowly, he watched the boy closely as he said deliberately, "and this is Miss Sarah Swanson from England."

Not a flicker of recognition crossed the boy's face, he neither remembered Sarah or the name.

"Nice to meet you."

Sarah found herself looking into her father's laughing blue eyes, "Robert," Sarah was at a loss to say more, she had never given a thought to the children not knowing her. "Mary" she faltered, "where is Mary?"

"Bring Mary from indoors please Robert." Rachel Cameron had reappeared bearing a large pitcher of iced lemon.

Robert obediently left the company to reappear shortly afterwards hand in hand with a younger child, too young to be Sarah's sister, for Mary Ann was the Swanson's second eldest.

"This is Mary," Andrew placed an affectionate arm about the child, anyone seeing the striking likeness of the ginger haired couple would be right to assume they were father and daughter.

Sarah concealed her disappointment and later waved Josh goodbye, she had accepted Andrew Cameron's kind offer.

A mixture of feelings beset Sarah in the course of the next few days, she was to witness the great bond of love between Robert and the Camerons. She had an overwhelming urge to seize her brother and demand his return, then her ardour weakened when Rachel recalled how the English children had brought untold joy to herself and her husband. They had tried in vain to conceive a child, after ten years of failure they had been blessed with two adopted children. They thought their family complete when two years later Rachel became pregnant, the wording of her next statement did not go unnoticed by Sarah.

"The baby brought great joy to my children, our elder daughter had never really settled, time and time again she would go missing only to be found each time at the docks, but when the baby was expected she was delighted and settled down. We found her to be an extremely intelligent girl, so much so that although we were heartbroken to part with her we allowed her to go off to residential college; she hopes to become a school teacher, but we do have her home most weekends. Sarah noted the woman's radiance when speaking of the children, she seemed especially fond of Robert. Agonising decisions consumed Sarah, she lay awake at night fiercely defending her rights, the children were hers, the same blood ran in their veins, she prayed to her parents for guidance to help her find a way to ease the Cameron's distress. It was Robert who was to be the one to make Sarah realize the only decision.

A number of people had come to the Cameron home to meet the lady from (what they called) the old country. After their departure Sarah came upon Robert sitting on a fence, he surprised her by saying, "I was born in the old country."

"Yes Robert, I know you were."

"I don't know what part though, could be London where the king lives."

"No, you were born in a lovely place called Kent."

"How do you know that?"

"Because I was born there."

"Did you know my English ma and pa?"

Sarah thought her heart would burst, she felt a surge of respect for the Camerons, at least they had not pretended to the boy.

"Yes Robert I did," she hesitated then took the plunge,

"they were my ma and pa also."

The boy looked at her with wrinkled forehead. "Does that mean I am your brother?"

"Yes" the word was breathed quietly.

A beaming smile greeted her answer.

"Great, that means I have three sisters, not two."

He leapt from the fence and raced excitedly towards the house calling "come on."

Sarah followed him laughing

"Where to? Where are you going?"

"To tell my ma and pa of course."

Most of Sarah's remaining time was taken up telling Robert of his English family. When he heard his English father had been a ship's captain his eyes rounded as if listening to a fairy tale.

When Josh arrived Sarah was surrounded by a happy household. She was in the car ready to depart with Mary Ann's address in her handbag when Rachel said suddenly "Mary Ann insisted on changing her name."

"Oh, what name did she take?"

Sarah was shocked at the reply.

"Ruth."

The day before Sarah's early morning departure from Canada she faced the sullen figure in the college grounds.

"You knew didn't you? Why on earth didn't you speak up?"

The blonde teenager's head jerked up, stormy eyes centred on Sarah, "why should I, you didn't even recognize me."

Sarah interrupted in amazement, "you were a ten year old,

you're a strong healthy sixteen year old now, nothing like the little slim girl I remembered, even your hair is a different colour."

"Well I don't care anymore, I'm a Canadian, you go home and keep your England, I'm going to be a teacher, and I'll be a good one. Do you think I'd have been given that opportunity in your England? You can keep it, what kind of a country palms their children off into strange lands? I don't want any part of it, you like it, well you get back there."

Sarah's heart sank on hearing the bitterness, she whispered "Oh Mary Ann we were heartbroken, we were powerless."

"Oh were you, don't you talk to me about heartbreak, do you think it was joy that made me keep returning to the docks?" Her eyes spat fire, "I used to watch people disembarking in the hope someone had come for me. Well I don't need you now, I took that job in the dock office for a few hours a week just so I could be reminded what England had done by looking at that damned dock shed."

A grief stricken Sarah could only murmur brokenly "Oh Mary Ann."

"Don't call me that," the voice reached near hysteria, my name is Ruth Cameron, and I *am* a Canadian."

The girl suddenly sprinted across the grounds and disappeared indoors.

The following morning Josh arrived early, he hid his dismay at Sarah's impending departure. While he kept up a one sided cheerful conversation, a sad Sarah paid little attention. On arrival at the docks Sarah suddenly left Josh to take care of her luggage when she spied the young figure sitting on the ground near the dock shed. As she drew near the blonde head was lowered, the girl appeared to be examining the ground. Sarah thought of her own heartache between the ages of thirteen and sixteen, scalding tears smarted her eyes, she sobbed out one whispered word, "Please."

The head was slowly raised, the girl's lovely face was puffed, her large blue eyes looked up at Sarah, a torrent of tears rained down her cheeks, she said brokenly "Sarah why didn't mummy come with you?"

Sarah leaned down and swept the youngster in a fierce embrace.

"Oh, Mary Ann, Ruthie it doesn't matter what you call yourself you are still my sister and I love you."

The sisters clung together sobbing.

Two short hours later Sarah smiled through her tears as she waved goodbye. She was happy, for her sister had begged her to return; the bitterness towards England had not changed and she preferred to be addressed as Ruth, she still insisted she was Canadian but she had admitted her love for her family had never left her. Sarah had promised over and over to return.

Chapter 12

The best at being good

Only Tom and Miriam had set up home away from Clare St., the rest were so comfortable they had no wish to leave, but this evening Esther was in her element, all her family were together for Sarah's home coming.

Intense attention was paid as Sarah told of her travels, worried frowns met the news that only two children had been sent to Canada. Josh had been adamant the authorities had no knowledge of the other two children.

"We'll find them girl, our Tom'll make enquiries won't y' lad, but c'mon now dinner's ready. Sarah put the cloth on th' table an get th' knives n' forks out th' drawer there's a good girl." Sarah smiled as she did Esther's bidding, she treasured the woman who had befriended her mother and still treated her as she had on their first meeting. Sarah doubted she would ever be an adult in Esther's eyes.

Having served everyone and satisfied herself they all had enough on their plates Esther said suddenly, "it's a shame about poor Kate McKeva isn't it?"

Sarah felt fear clutch her heart.

"Why?" Sarah was terrified of what answer her question would reveal but she forced herself to ask, "what's happened? Is she alright?"

"No girl, she's not well at all, took t' her bed and won't even answer the door, no-one's seen sight n'sign of her f'days now.

Edward went away a few days ago an' I think Kate took bad soon after."

Sarah sprang to her feet, "I'm sorry, I must go to her right away."

She left the startled company and sped off hurriedly towards Gerard St., she didn't bother to knock but called loudly through the letter box "Kate, Kate, it's me Sarah, open the door."

A shuffling came from within, then the door slowly opened, the woman stood in the hallway bent and old, her lips trembled, she looked pitiful. "I knew y'd' come," she laid her head on Sarah's shoulder as loving arms embraced her.

"Oh Kate," they clung together until Sarah led her old friend through to the back room, without speaking she stoked up the dying red embers of the fire. It wasn't until she handed Kate a steaming cup of tea that she broke the silence, her voice was unusually demanding, "what's the matter with you? Why aren't you looking after yourself?"

Kate's voice was tearful, "what's th'use? There's no-one left t'look after no more. Maggie Ellen's gone, an Edward's gonna sell up, he's gettin' rid of all the houses an's talkin' about signin' on in the army f'twenty one years."

"Why would he want to do that?" Sarah was truly mystified as to why a man on the brink of marriage would contemplate such a step.

"He's changed Sarah, he's not the happy lad that went off t' Egypt. He came back here the other week as miserable as sin an' he's never been the same since. I don't know if he's missin' his mam or what but I don't like it, he won't talk t'me no more. He just stood in the doorway lookin' at his mother's houses, then he couldn't even do that no more when the street suddenly come a parade ground f'all the neighbourhood girls." Kate gave a deep sigh, "I might as well give up n'die quietly with no fuss."

"I've never heard anything so stupid Kate McKeva, now buck up and stop all this nonsense or I'll move in here and make you. What of Lilli anyway? What's happened to her?"

"Good riddance t' that one, she's led poor Edward a right dance. He's even had t'go on th' train t'take her home, said she was too scared t'travel by herself, I don't know when Edward will get back, poor lad."

Sarah sniffed unkindly, she didn't see anything poor about him, he had probably used the blonde, and for all the moaning about her he seemed to have enjoyed Lilli's company.

"Come on Kate, let's make you comfortable and I'll leave you to rest."

"Ah no Sarah, y' only just come, stay an' talk t'me, I want t'know what y've been doin, y' looks lovely." Kate coaxed "stay a bit longer, tell me about Canada."

"Alright just a little while."

Sarah started to speak of her travels. Kate wriggled herself more comfortable and leaned forward listening eagerly, her eyes took on their old sparkle. Sarah continued with tales of her work and the factory.

Kate interrupted, "It's wonderful what y'v done f'people, y'a good girl."

When Sarah blushed and tried to sweep aside the compliment Kate protested "oh I know what y'v done, I saw it every day with me own eyes, pity that Lilli couldn't do somethin' better with her time."

Sarah spoke quietly, "she is very very beautiful Kate."

"They all were Sarah, but where she gets that fair hair an' white skin from is a mystery, the rest was all dark. Maggie Ellen's mam and dad and their brothers an' sisters were all dark haired, Maggie Ellen an Edward as well, even Carl who's her half brother is dark."

Sarah was speechless.

"She came here for her Auntie Maggie Ellen's funeral an' f'got t' go back home till a few days ago."

The room filled with the sound of whimpering. A shocked Kate looked as tears tumbled down Sarah's face, she immediately returned to her old self and addressed Sarah as a babe.

"Child what's th' matter w'y', has someone hurt y'again." Her face became thunderous, "I'll kill them, now do as y'told an' tell me who's hurt y'."

"No, no Kate," Sarah shook her head as she cried aloud like a broken-hearted child.

Kate rose from her seat, she stood tall and straight her fists clenched hard, "Tell me" she roared, "God forgive me I'll kill them."

With her back to the door the distraught Sarah was unaware it had opened until Kate begged.

"Edward help her lad."

Edward had entered the house unheard above all the shouting and weeping. He looked tired.

Sarah spun about to face the figure framed in the doorway, they stood spellbound looking at each other. Sarah's face crumpled, "I didn't know she was your cousin."

Edward slowly held out his arms and as Sarah rushed into them he gave a deep sigh of contentment, he closed his eyes and lay his tanned face against her hair.

Kate was mystified but she looked on beaming.

The following morning Kate stood framed in the same doorway, she demanded to know, "have youse two stayed up all night?" Edward snuggled Sarah deeper into his arms, his twinkling blue eyes smiled up at Kate, "I made her stay to tell me her life story, and tonight I'm going to tell her mine."

"She already knows it."

Sarah laughed, "Kate has told me what a perfect baby you were, in fact she told me many times."

Edward put on a mock thoughtful expression, he mimicked a child, "Well, I'll tell her about Egypt."

"She knows that too," Kate wore a satisfied smirk.

Edward raised his eyebrows.

"Who d'y think read y'letters t'y'mother n'me, an' who d'y' think wrote all them there letters t'y'."

Sarah giggled and nodded in answer to his unasked question, her eyes were laughing shimmering pools.

Kate snorted, "Y' don't think she'd kiss a feller she didn't know, d' y'? Y' t' be good t'her Edward, I don't want no nonsense, she's suffered enough through your family."

"Kate please," Edward's arms tightened as Sarah showed signs of distress.

"Alright I'll keep me mouth shut, but y't' take care of her Edward, I mean it now."

"Yes Kate I hear you," Edward was suddenly serious, he was later to question Kate at great length.

"Now it's no good y'wastin' time sittin' there I've got a job y'both can do." Kate disappeared.

Edward whispered in Sarah's ear, "You certainly left your mark on Kate."

Sarah answered softly before he kissed her, "I hope as deeply as she left hers on me."

"Here y'are, make y'selves busy sortin' that lot," she placed a jewel box alongside them on the sofa, "it's stuff y'mother collected from Berry's, see what y'want t'keep Edward an' I'll sell the rest back t' them."

The opened lid revealed Maggie Ellen's sparkling jewels.

"Is there anything there you would like Sarah?"

She shook her head quickly before replying "no thank you Edward, I couldn't, really."

He looked tenderly at her lowered head and suddenly closed the box, "I'll sort this out later," then he turned to Kate, "Sarah won't be staying tonight Kate, she has to be up early tomorrow morning."

Kate nodded her satisfaction.

Edward cupped Sarah's crestfallen face in his hands, he whispered gently, "You have played truant today Sarah, go to work tomorrow," his lip's brushed hers, "I will be there to see you home."

A disappointed Sarah gave a resigned sigh, she did not see the look of approval Edward was awarded from Kate.

The following two weeks were a whirl of happiness. Sarah's face took on a radiant beauty that had she but known it far outclassed her steble fountain ladies. Edward was there promptly every evening to meet her at the factory, he accompanied her on her train journeys. The delighted Tylers insisted the couple stayed overnight and Cathrine arrived to complete Desmond and his parent's joy. Sarah was ecstatic, all the people she held so dear rejoiced in her happiness, only a slight uneasiness marred Sarah's blissful state. Edward would gently insist their evenings ended at a reasonable time, so much so she was disturbed by thoughts of whether or not he really cared for her. She refused to become miserable when these thoughts persisted. His decision to leave the army brought untold relief, Sarah's agonies of ever having to part were dismissed. Edward had also decided to dispense with his mother's properties.

Then Mark and Estelle's wedding day arrived, Sarah found herself acting as bridesmaid once more. The service was lovely and the reception afterwards was the best ever. Sarah could not resist the temptation of speaking to the Adelphi manager, shortly afterwards a beaming chef was allowed to join the celebrations. After a joyous reunion Sarah introduced him to the French guests, in fact the whole proceedings had a French air, for Yvette's family had joined Estelle's relations for their visit.

With suspiciously bright eyes Esther counted her blessings, three marriages had brought her three wonderful daughters. She smiled happily as Sarah glided by in Edward's arms, she was pleased she had no worries about the handsome couple. She remembered a very different Edward, his good looks had always attracted females and it was the army that put a halt to the expectations of his becoming the neighbourhood romeo. Sarah was happy and that completed Esther's contentment.

Floating in Edward's arms Sarah wondered why he seemed preoccupied. He had been happy and relaxed until Jim O'Niel had handed him an envelope.

"Edward would you rather we leave now? You don't seem to be enjoying yourself."

She felt his arms tighten slightly about her and was surprised when he led her off the dance floor. He kept walking until the wedding reception was left behind then he guided her to a quiet corner of the lounge. His blue eyes searched her face, holding both her hands he looked earnestly into her eyes, she had never seen him so serious.

"Sarah, this relationship of ours, is it as important to you as it is to me?"

Sarah's heart beat crazily, she was taken off guard.

He rushed on not waiting for a reply, "I have been acting like a schoolboy Sarah, I've been so terrified of losing you, I have done my utmost to court you properly, the thought that you would liken me to Carl almost drove me crazy. I don't know what I did wrong at our first meeting but when you ran away from me I hung about your flat for days, then the workmen told me you had moved out. I didn't know where you had gone, in desperation I approached Tom, your attack on him left me in no doubt you didn't want to know me." His voice dropped to a troubled whisper, "Sarah I love you, I have loved you ever since the first evening I walked you home from Tom's wedding."

As much as she longed to hear his words Sarah placed fingers tenderly across his lips, a nervous giggle escaped her, he looked dejected, then she breathed, "Edward I have loved you since the night before you left for Egypt."

"*Sarah,*" he raised his head and gave a stunned relieved laugh. "Darling Sarah marry me, say you will marry me."

Tears of joy threatened as Sarah nodded eagerly. They clung together deliriously happy.

"Let's tell Esther, Oh Edward let's tell everyone."

He lovingly traced her lips with a finger before replying "you had better warn them the wedding will be soon."

"How soon," Sarah was in seventh heaven.

"Very, very soon, I have tickets booked on a liner."

Sarah came down to earth, she said in stunned tones, "you have tickets for *what?*"

"Let me tell you what has happened first, I had Jim O'Niel do some detecting for me," Edward took an envelope from his pocket, "as you now know one of your sisters and a brother were sent to Canada; Sarah the other two were kept here, Alec was sent to Hightown in Formby, and Agnes was placed in a convent a few miles away.

Sarah was flabbergasted, all this time she had been separated from her brother and sister by only a few miles.

Edward shook her playfully and laughed, "Sarah if we go as a married couple the children will be released. The tickets are booked for twelve weeks time, let's get the kids and use the voyage for our honeymoon."

A starry-eyed Sarah was speechless.

Losing no time Hightown was paid a visit the very next day. With her heart thumping madly Sarah ran along the highly polished floorboards to keep up with Edward and a school official, their reception had left her apprehensive. The disciplinary manner which met their enquiries prompted Edward's demand to see the school's principal whose manner proved more comforting than those of his underling. After lending a sympathetic ear he warned them a higher authority would have to be consulted.

"Please, will you allow me to see Alex?"

The man smiled at Sarah's tenseness, "Yes Miss Swanson, I think that would be in order, but I hope you will agree it would not be advisable the boy should meet you until we have definite news for him."

Sarah replied with a hurried whisper, "yes, yes of course you are right, but please allow me to see him now."

Holding Edward's hand tightly she followed the school's headmaster into a large hall, she held her breath as she witnessed about thirty boys prepare for choir practice, her eyes sped frantically over the youngster's faces when a kindly voice said in her ear, "your brother is the boy on the end of the first row."

She looked at the figure the man indicated and marvelled at the transformation; the last time she had seen him he was a six year old tousle haired bare footed boy. Alex was now a sturdy twelve year old, his skin shone with cleanliness, like the other boys he wore grey trousers and a spotless white shirt which was topped by a broad stiff collar, his legs were clad in knee high grey socks and sturdy shoes.

"Oh he looks wonderful, look Edward isn't he lovely."

As the boy's voices rang out in song Sarah was led out of the room, her eyes were shining. "Thank you, oh thank you, you will let us meet soon won't you?"

With the sound of a sincere promise ringing in her ears Sarah went happily in search of her sister.

Access to the convent proved more difficult. After three days of trying to speak to someone through a small flap in the front door Sarah was advised to contact the authorities. The search reminded Sarah of when the children were first taken away, she and Edward met with denials of responsibility. Eventually Esther approached the Canon of her church, her pleadings proved successful for an appointment was made allowing one visitor to the convent.

A week later Sarah approached the main entrance again, she was surprised when the heavy door swung open after only one bang on the large brass knocker, observers had gone unseen. Without a word a nun bowed her head to the visitor, then with a rustling of her sombre robes she walked quickly down a stone floor corridor. Sarah followed until she was silently ushered into a room. As she noted the sparse furnishing Sarah was startled when a voice said,

"Miss Swanson?"

Sarah peered at the figure in the shadows.

"Yes, I am Sarah Swanson."

"Have you any proof of who you say you are?"

Sarah felt a surge of anger, "I beg your pardon," her whole body bristled.

"You must understand we are very protective of our children, we don't allow just anyone to enter and try to contact them."

"I am well aware of that, I have wasted a lot of time just trying to get into this place."

"This place as you call it Miss Swanson has provided a good home for your sister," the voice was without anger but firm as it continued "the girl may become unsettled, she is perfectly happy here, she will soon be of an age to take instruction."

Sarah looked bewildered, "instruction in what?"

"Agnes has declared an interest in becoming a nun."

Sarah looked horrified, "but she's only fifteen."

"The child is quite happy with her life at the convent."

Sarah's face grew pale, she asked quietly "can I see her please?"

"No I'm afraid not, little use would come of unsettling her now."

"She's my sister, she must leave here, I want her with me."

"Miss Swanson," the voice became reasoning, "I couldn't possibly release her to an unattached young lady."

"I'm to be married very soon, oh please allow me to see her."
"Even so proof of your marriage would be needed and no I cannot allow a visit which may prove upsetting for her, I am sorry." The nun rang a small handbell, the door opened immediately. "Yes Reverend Mother?" the novice at the door was little more than an obedient teenager.

"Miss Swanson is leaving now sister."

The Mother Superior smiled gently and bid Sarah goodbye before leaving the room.

In a daze Sarah found herself outside, on seeing the pallor of her face, a worried looking Edward rushed forward to meet her.

"Edward, they wouldn't let me see her."

Comforting arms embraced her as tears glinted in her eyes. "Agnes is going to be a nun" she whispered, "oh Edward she's only a child."

"They wouldn't force her Sarah, they wouldn't even ask her, she must have approached the subject herself. Don't upset yourself darling, perhaps it's what she really wants."

"But Edward how can she be certain? She is so young." Sarah buried her face in his chest and sobbed "I wasn't even allowed to see her, oh Edward I was in the same building, so close and yet I didn't even see her."

"Come on now, let's get home and discuss this, there must be something we can do." Edward dabbed her eyes with his handkerchief, "we will find a way for you two to meet somehow."

That evening Esther's house echoed with raised voices, although the whole family were frequent churchgoers they were angry. Esther sped off to see the Canon, she was going to demand to know why Agnes was not allowed visitors.

The Canon returned with her, he had christened all three and married two of Esther's sons and held a strong liking for the family. He placed a hand on the sobbing Sarah's head, then while Esther made a pot of tea he appeased,

"Come now child, don't upset y'self, it's not the devil your sisters going t'meet." He was loathe to admit the church's involvement in the confiscation of the children.

Sarah knew the man, she had held many conversations with him in the past.

"Canon, they didn't believe me, I was even asked for identification."

"Well crying won't get you anywhere Sarah, let me see now, would you have your sister's birth certificate?"

"No," Sarah raised a worried face.

"Well no matter, no matter now, we will write off for a copy, then I can approach the Bishop with some proof. Where you christened at the same church? A copy of yours would be a help as well."

"Yes," Sarah nodded eagerly.

"Good, good, y'see things are looking better already aren't they?" His eyes twinkled.

"Yes Canon," Sarah smiled through her tears.

"We'll get y' a visit at least, now what's the name and address of the church?"

"It wasn't a church Canon, it was a chapel."

The holy man looked at Sarah a little while before asking "what kind of a chapel child?"

"A Wesleyan chapel."

The whole household looked at each other with widened eyes. The priest said slowly "Sarah are you telling me you and your sisters are Methodists?"

With faltering tones Sarah answered quietly "yes Canon." She wondered why Edward and the three O'Halleron brothers suddenly roared with laughter, Mark sprayed the company with a mouthful of tea, Esther roared at him to show more respect. The old priest put his head in his hands for a moment then after blessing himself he said "Holy Mary mother of God," he got speedily to his feet, "I'll be back t'see y' tomorrow Sarah," he left the house quicker than he came in.

Sarah felt silly when the laughter makers explained, for she had never given a thought to her sister being a non-Catholic.

Two days later the girls were reunited. The Canon accompanied Sarah to the convent; on the way he explained, the parish from where the children were taken was predominantly Catholic, no-one had questioned the children's religions, the convent had acted in good faith. Their aim was solely to protect Agnes, but on finding that a letter (if one was forthcoming) from a non-Catholic Bishop would almost certainly obtain the girl's release they had decided to allow Agnes her freedom.

As they entered the vestibule a young figure rose to meet them, she was dressed for outdoors, she looked at Sarah with uncertainty, "Sarah? Are you Sarah?"

Unable to speak Sarah swallowed a huge lump in her throat as she nodded.

The quiet voice continued, but this time it was joyous "Why didn't you let me know you were coming?"

"Didn't anyone tell you?"

Agnes shook her head.

"But how did you know me?"

"Your eyes Sarah, they were always just like mummy's."

"Oh Agnes."

The two sister's fell into each others arms and held on tightly. The old priest wept on witnessing the reunion.

A week later Sarah's happiness was made complete on being informed Alex would be allowed to attend her wedding and all haste would be made in transferring guardianship to her and her husband.

A few weeks later the bridal couple stood at the ship's rail, an excited Alex and Agnes had raced down to their cabins as soon as they boarded. The blissful couple roared with laughter as a tall gaunt figure caused a commotion on the dock side, a six foot baggage handler was sent sprawling for daring to bar her way. Looking unusual in a wide brimmed hat and a long black coat Kate McKeva climbed the gangplank, her eyes were gleaming, she was going to enjoy taking care of the newlyweds.

In all her radiance Sarah immediately closed her eyes at her beloved's request, the facing of her suit took his attention, then after brushing her lips with his he whispered, "I found this amongst my mother's jewellery, will you wear it for me?"

Sarah looked down at the gold entwined hearts.

Edward said huskily "S for Sarah and E for Edward, you will wear it won't you darling?"

A blissful smile spread over her face, she heard her father's loving tones, "E for Edith and S for Sam," then she replied "Yes, oh my darling yes, I'll wear it always."

With his lips touching her cheek Edward whispered "I love you, are you happy Sarah?"

Eyes sparkling she breathed "Oh darling no-one has ever been more so, I love you so very much."

Kate went unheard as she said "Maggie Ellen took a fancy t' that brooch in Berry's, them were her mam n' dad's initials," her eyes took on a contented look as she beheld the blissful couple. Sarah and Edward were oblivious to all as they lovingly embraced. As the ship got under way she turned in his arms and watched the receding of the Liverpool skyline. "I love your city Edward, I don't think I'd have survived elsewhere."

He laughed and put on an arrogant skittish nasal accent, "didn't y'know girl we're the best at everythin'." Then he grew serious. "Unfortunately like everwhere else we have our undesirables and those few can be bad."

Before replying Sarah centred her eyes on the Royal Liver Building. She thought of the Adelphi chef and Eve, of the wholesale market traders and Jim O'Niel, the Rabbi and the kind Joe Silver, of Maggie Ellen and Kate and finally of Esther and her sons. Then she said softly, "Yes my love, but the rest are the best at being good."